PhotoDiary

Lynn Goldsmith

RIZZOLI
NEW YORK

First published in the United States of America in 1995 by
Rizzoli International Publications, Inc.
300 Park Avenue South, New York, NY 10010

Goldsmith, Lynn.
    Photodiary / Lynn Goldsmith.
        p.   cm.
    ISBN 0-8478-1876-4 (hc). — ISBN 0-8478-1883-7 (pb)
    1. Rock musicians—United States—Portraits. 2. Portrait
photography—United States. 3. Rock music—United States—History
and criticism. 4. Goldsmith, Lynn.
    TR681.M86G65 1995
    779' .2'092—dc20   95-5164
                                                        CIP

Designed by Ron Meckler, Re:Design, New York

Printed and bound in Japan

This book is dedicated to the person
who told me getting married and
having children was not for every girl.
She said, "Travel, meet people, and
live, live, live!" Thanks Mom.

PhotoDiary

Lynn Goldsmith

a wop bop alu bop

Dad does a swan dive

I was born on February 11th, 1948, in Detroit, Michigan. My mom was a housewife and my dad an engineer. My dad had dreamed of doing swan dives off cliffs in Mexico. I think my mom wanted to be some kind of star because she always dressed like one. I thought my sister, Ellen, who was four years older than me, was a beautiful princess. She was delicate, with blond hair and blue eyes. She was always clean. I had dark brown hair, green eyes, and was always dirty. They called me butterball because I'd grab any available stick of butter and shove it into my mouth. Needless to say, I was chubby. Over my right eye hung a purple blood clot. Basically, I used my left eye to see the world around me. I knew there was something wrong with the way I looked because when my dad took my picture, he'd tell me to turn profile.

Mom, Me, and Ellen

At the age of four, I was sent to overnight summer camp with my sister. I was the youngest kid there.

Every night I'd cry because I missed my mom. The cabin counselor would carry me out of my bunk into a rocking chair where she'd sing me to sleep. Her voice took away my loneliness, filling the void with love songs. This might have been the first connection I made to music melting away my fears. When I returned home, at the end of the summer, I remember running upstairs to look for my Dad. He was nowhere to be found. I opened up his closet. It was empty. My mom gently informed me they had gotten divorced.

It was arranged for Ellen and me to spend weekends with him. That fall I entered kindergarten at MacDowell Elementary. I'd had radium treatment for the blood clot over my eye, so now I just had a big space in my eyebrow. I'd lost my appetite after my dad had gone and I'd become so skinny kids called me "Lynn The Pin." Like half of the kids in school, I was white and Jewish. The other half were black Christians. No one in my class had divorced parents. Sometimes I felt ashamed of it. My mom got a job to support us. Ellen and I now spent more time at my grandparents. Their neighborhood was at least 60% black. I never thought America was anything but black

a wop bam boom!

and white. When I came home from school, our housekeeper, Shirlee, who was black, would turn on the radio and dance with me. I was seven years old when I heard Fats Domino's "All By Myself." Something connected. When I heard Little Richard's "Tutti-Frutti," something ignited. I'd park myself in front of my mom's dressing mirror and sing

Nanny and Papa

into it for hours. I really loved Little Richard. Around the time I turned eight he released "Long Tall Sally," and I went nuts. As soon as he hit the first note, I'd run as fast as I could in circles through the house. From the hallway to the kitchen to the den to the living room and back to the hallway, round and round. When I stopped, breathless, I'd slam my head against the wall to the beat of the song. You might say I was the first "headbanger." My mom would scream at me to stop. I promised I would if she'd buy the record and a record player. Not having a father around made it easier to get what I wanted. The big disappointment was that the record player was put in her bedroom. This meant I had to ask permission to use it. When I look back, I think she might have put it in her bedroom because she wanted to listen to music before she went to sleep, but at that time I was sure she kept

it there so she could control me. As soon as I got home from school, I'd run upstairs to her room and put on my forty-fives. I'd gotten her to buy "Blueberry Hill" by Fats, "Speedoo" by the Cadillacs, "Earth Angel" by the Penguins, and "A Thousand Miles Away" by the Heartbeats. It didn't bother me so much anymore that my sister didn't want to play with me when she had friends around, because I had my music. I'd dance with the closet doorknob to "Get a Job," "Book of Love," and "Searchin'." My mom bought me a red-and-black case to keep my forty-five collection together. When I opened it, Elvis's newest single, "Love Me Tender," was inside. She'd hum that song and I'd know we understood each other in a special way.

Camp Tanuga

In 1957, my mom decided to move to Hollywood, Florida. We rented our house, packed the car, drove all night, and ended up in an all-white neighborhood inhabited by people so different from us that I believed they must have come from another planet. My sister changed her name to Bunny. She didn't want any of her new classmates knowing she was Jewish. We shared a house with mom's business partner, Audrey, who was divorced with

Ninth Grade, 1961

two daughters around the same age as Ellen and me. Neither of them knew about Little Richard, much less the Coasters, the Olympics, or the Fleetwoods. I think I survived because of American Bandstand. Everybody on that show loved music and they knew how to dance. They were my friends.

Mom and Audrey had a shop with stuff like motorized, jeweled flashlight fans, insect pins with moving rhinestone antennae, beaded clutch purses, etc., etc.. Everything was really expensive. The problem was that this Hollywood wasn't in California. It was one of the poorer parts of Florida. I don't know what my mom was thinking. They went out of business within a year. We packed up, got back in the car, and returned to our house in Detroit.

My dad had gotten married and moved to Houston, Texas. Summers were spent with him and his new wife. On the buses were signs, "Blacks To The Back," and over drinking fountains—"For Colored," or "For Whites Only." The six o'clock TV movies featured stories where the South won the Civil War. I was very confused. I'd scour my dad's morning paper looking for some word on Elvis. Whenever they took us out to eat, Paul Anka's "Diana" was on the jukebox. I figured out how to play it on a ukulele my dad had. They'd ask me to sing for their friends. I liked performing, but I

wanted to sing like Little Richard and they didn't like that.

On my tenth birthday I got a turquoise transistor radio. Now I could take music with me everywhere. Turning the volume up as far as it would go, pushing my ear tightly against the speaker, listening to "To Know Him Is To Love Him" by the Teddy Bears or "I Love You So" by the Chantels, I'd be transported into what felt like another dimension. I no longer missed my mom, who wasn't home like other moms because she was working, nor did I miss my dad, who lived too far away for any weekend visits. I wanted more than ever for my sister to be friends with me. She looked like Justine, one of the most popular girls on American Bandstand, only prettier. I had become a good dancer, so sometimes if I showed her friends my latest steps, she'd let me join them. I'd even sing "I Met Him on a Sunday" by the Shirelles or "Who's Sorry Now" by Connie Francis for them.

I wanted to be a singer. I thought one day I might get to sing with Elvis. My heart broke when Elvis went into the army. I told my grandpa about my desires and he said, "Show business...phooey." A little spit came out when he said "phooey." He told my mother that I had to start going to temple. The first Saturday I heard the rabbi speak, he told the story of the Tower of Babel. The people wanted to get to Heaven so they started building a tower up into the sky. When they got too close, God stopped them by giving them different languages. They couldn't build any higher because they couldn't speak to each other. I thought, Why didn't they just sing? For me, music could solve anything. It went beyond words. It went beyond age. It made everybody one.

When I was thirteen, my mom got married again. We moved to Miami Beach, Florida. I wasn't real happy about it, but I knew she was tired of working and happy to have someone strong love her. He wanted me to like him so he bought me a "princess" canopy bed set. He also wanted me to know that now I had a "father" who was going to give me some "needed" discipline. If I didn't "tow the line," which in this case meant eating vegetables at least three times a week, keeping my room clean, and turning lights off, then I wasn't allowed to play my records. I hated him that first year and escaped into the TV. The biggest influence on me other than music, up to that point in my life, was the Fred Astaire films shown on the tube. Those movies made me believe Mr. Right would know beyond any doubt he had met Miss Right (and vice versa) the moment their eyes met. They were fated to be together forever. I thought life would probably have a happy ending because Astaire movies always had happy endings.

At fourteen my life changed. I heard Bob Dylan. His songs made me feel there is no Mr. Right for Miss Right. In fact, there is no Mr. or Miss Right at all. There

Miami Beach High, 1964

is no everlasting happiness. Life is not about bad times or good times. Dylan made me feel being alive was more about seeing my own life as a chance to learn and that whatever emotion I might feel was temporary. I don't think I verbalized it like that then, but I convinced my mom to get me a sunburst Gibson guitar. I wrote a song about racism in the land of the free and the brave. My sister, Ellen, now eighteen, would sneak me out of the house after my mother and stepfather went to bed. She'd drive to coffee houses in Coconut Grove and push me up on the stage. I'd sing my songs about Jim Crow. I never really knew if the audience liked the songs. I felt they were entertained because there didn't seem to be anyone around as little as me with such a big guitar, singin' songs about the struggles of the black man.

I missed Detroit. The Marvelettes did "Please Mr. Postman" and I'd sit in my room and cry. The cutest boy in Miami Beach High School, Miles, decided he was in love with me. The Marvelettes put out "Playboy" and Mary Wells did "Two Lovers," songs that told me not to trust men. Perfect timing. I knew to act hard to get with a guy like Miles. This made him crazy for me. It also somehow made me popular in school. I was asked to be a cheerleader!

When 1964 rolled in, everything was pretty exciting. The Beatles were going to kick off their American invasion in Miami Beach. My stepfather had

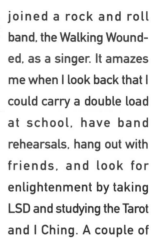

My Band, 1967

gotten me into the lobby of the hotel they were arriving at and tickets for the Ed Sullivan show. I'd become a Rolling Stones fan with "Not Fade Away," and the Beatles to me were goody-goodies. I went just to please my stepfather. Before the Beatles came on stage I thought all the screaming girls were idiots. Then they hit the first note and I was standing on my chair like the rest of them, tears running down my face, screaming, "George, George." I really didn't understand then or now the emotions that swept over me. As '64 and '65 brought hit after hit from the Beatles, I came to love them.

At seventeen, I left Miami to go to the University of Michigan. My sister now lived in New York. She was an artist (painter) by day and a waitress at Max's Kansas City at night. Her boyfriend was in the Velvet Underground and she was in Andy Warhol's circle. I spent three days there with her before starting school in Ann Arbor. I knew I wanted to graduate as soon as possible and live in New York, too. I made the decision to get my degree in three years. I doubled the normal credit load. After the first year, I joined a rock and roll band, the Walking Wounded, as a singer. It amazes me when I look back that I could carry a double load at school, have band rehearsals, hang out with friends, and look for enlightenment by taking LSD and studying the Tarot and I Ching. A couple of times the Walking Wounded got gigs in New York.

In Manhattan, we met a band called Children of Paradise. One day they came to Ann Arbor and called me. After their show, I drove them in my car to an area which was reported to have flying saucer landings. We were driving slowly looking for the saucers when we got pulled over by the police. I was unaware that my guests had stuck their pot under my front car seat. The police searched the car and arrested all of us. At the station, the Children of Paradise said the marijuana was mine. They just wanted to get back to New York and left me to take the rap. I was charged with a felony and spent five days in jail before being bailed out. I was allowed one phone call a day. Each day I'd call one of my parents. My father thought my mother was coming for me and he didn't want to see her, and my mom thought my father was coming and she didn't want to see him. So they just left me there thinking that the other one was coming for me. I remember singing "Chain of Fools" and "Do Right Woman, Do Right Man" softly in my cell. I didn't know

Ann Arbor, 1966

Street Peddler, 1970

all the words, but pretending I was Aretha Franklin made me feel less scared. Finally, my stepfather, George, got on a plane and came and got me out. He asked me to tell him about my history with drugs. I told the truth. I had smoked dope, eaten mushrooms, and taken acid many times for "higher learning" purposes. I was over that stage and was now into purification of the body and macrobiotics. He put his head into his hands and wept. "Your brain, Lynnie, your brain. What have you done to your brain?" I thought, "What did I do to my brain?" He wanted me to promise to quit my band and to return home to Miami for a minimum of six months to be an English teacher when I graduated. He made it clear he would not pay for the attorney if I argued with his request. John Sinclair had just been sentenced in Michigan to ten years in prison for one joint. I decided it was in my best interest to make the promise.

Over the next year, a misdemeanor was negotiated. I was given probation. In June of 1968 I graduated and was back at Miami Beach High as a substitute English teacher in the fall. As soon as the six months were up, I drove with friends to Los Angeles where my sister had moved with her new boyfriend Ralph, a piano player. They had a tiny place, but she let me stay with them. I wrote songs with Ralph, wore bells on my ankles, got "sha ka bu kued" into Nichiren Shoshu Buddhism, and realized that if I didn't move to New York my brain would shrink. Manhattan, 1969. I lied my way into a job for Elektra Records. I figured by the time they checked my resume, if they ever did, I'd have done so much good stuff for them that it wouldn't make a difference what I claimed to have done or not done in the past. I wanted to produce records. There were few, if any, female producers. Instead, I became a marketer of music, creating radio spots, print ads, and publicity campaigns.

After about two years, I was sick of the music business. I didn't want to sell music. I quit and became a street peddler. My friend made caricature Nixon and Agnew puppets and I sold them on the steps of the Episcopal Church on Fifth Avenue and 53rd Street every weekday from three to seven p.m. This gave me enough time and money for primal scream therapy. I thought self-investigation would bring a psychic healing. I felt a lot of anxiety because I wasn't sure what I wanted to be. I wasn't sure who I was. I didn't understand the way the world was. Everything had seemed so clear when I burned my bra on the library steps at Michigan or marched in Washington against the Vietnam War, but now it was 1971. Am I too old to be a rock and roller? Am I too young to get married? Do I

National Lampoon Photo Funnies

want to get married? What do I want to be? Who am I? Being a peddler gave me the time to think.

One afternoon I sold the puppets to a guy who worked for <u>National Lampoon</u> magazine. He suggested selling the puppets through them. I wasn't interested in making a career of selling puppets, but I was interested in the guy. I bought an issue and discov-

ered a section called Photo Funnies. Instead of illustrated cartoons, they were made up of pictures that told a story frame by frame. I thought, I can do that. Making photographs always came easy for me. Maybe because I was used to seeing the world through one eye, or maybe because when I was seven years old my father allowed me to go into the room behind the black velvet curtain.

Often I'd wondered what was going on in this special place he disappeared into for what seemed an eternity. The light was warm yellow. There was a big clock on the wall, the likes of which I'd never seen before. He picked me up, put me on a very tall stool, and made me promise to keep still. What happened in those next few moments remains so alive in my memory that I think there's a time warp where this scene is being played over and over. Very carefully, my father took a plain sheet of paper from a box and put it underneath some big rulers. Then he moved the hands on the big clock. He concentrated real hard as he moved his fingers around the white light coming from a tall machine. He smiled knowingly and told me to watch closely. He placed the paper in a tray filled with what I thought was water and flipped the paper from one side to the other, then jiggled it. I saw my own face appear on that very same piece of paper. In that moment, I knew for certain magic existed in the world. This was the proof! I wanted to make magic too, so he gave me a Baby Brownie camera.

My Baby Brownie

Directing California Jam with Joshua

So now at twenty-three, with no fear of making pictures, I borrowed a camera, wrote a story, and shot it using friends to act it out. I sold it to the <u>Lampoon</u>. I didn't think I was a professional photographer. I thought I had ideas which could be illustrated with pictures and that I could earn some money selling them. I had been taking pictures most of my life, but I never thought of it as a profession. I was still writing songs and working on who I was with psychotherapy and the I Ching. Then my sister Ellen came passing through New York on her way to London to join her boyfriend, Ralph, who was on the road with James Taylor. Somebody told her that when she got to New York she should call this guy, Joshua White, who was also on his way to London. He's the one who created the Joshua Light Show at the Fillmore East. His visuals were about as famous as the bands that played there. I went with my sister to the airport to see her off and meet Joshua. We fell in love on the spot. My life took a turn.

Joshua had just started his own company, Joshua TV. He did "video magnification." This meant large-screen projection for big rock acts. The rock and roll audience was now large enough to fill America's biggest venues, like Madison Square Garden and the Hollywood Bowl. He thought that in the not too distant future, rock concerts would be broadcast on network TV. Josh taught me how to direct and when ABC hired his company to produce the first in-concert shows, he got me into the Director's Guild. He also gave me his old Nikon FTN with a 50 mm lens. Having my own camera, I began to make more pictures. Josh and I didn't last long as lovers, but we did as friends and he changed my life.

Joshua assigned me to direct a short documentary on Grand Funk Railroad for ABC which provided the next turn of events. Grand Funk had been huge but their career was going downhill. They were selling half the amount of their earlier albums and had little remaining musical credibility. The press and radio were sick of them. It was at this unexpected moment when all my life experience came together. As if on fire, I told Andy Cavaliere, their manager, that Grand Funk should play off of being an American band. I said that it was time to put an end to the British music invasion. America needed to party with its own. I suggested they have Todd Rundgren produce. The press thought Todd was a genius and I knew radio would be receptive to listening to any record put together by this unlikely combo.

Todd and I had become good friends a few years before and I knew he needed the money Grand Funk could pay him. I declared they'd have a #1 single in all three trade magazines the same week if they did everything I suggested. I offered to work for nothing until that day. Then I would get a piece of the pie. Andy thought I was crazy, especially since Grand Funk had never had a hit single. They were an album band but I was so convincing, they went for it. Donny wrote the song "We're An American Band," Todd produced the album in ten days, and I designed a gold-foil record sleeve with a nude photo of the group inside and a logo that lit up under black light. I made a short film on them, radio spots, TV spots, and took lots of pictures to give to the magazines.

I moved through marketing/publicity ideas as though I was on a mission from God. I'll never forget the day <u>Record World</u>, <u>Cash Box</u>, and <u>Billboard</u> all had "We're An American Band" in the #1 spot. It reinforced for me that when the mind is focused on specific goals, there's a very good chance of success even when most people are telling you it's not possible. Todd produced the next album and I was still having fun doing things like the first 3-D album cover and stage clothes that lit up on their own. For the third album I wanted Fats Domino to be the producer. I thought the whole thing should be recorded in Fats's kitchen. The band, now secure with hit singles and albums behind them, was not so ready to do what I wanted. They had their own ideas. I felt I had accomplished what I set out to do and was ready to move on.

Although I continued photographing and consulting, my commitment changed. It was at this time that I met Hilda Charlton, a spiritual teacher. Meditation took a lot of time. I knew I could earn a living making pictures of musicians and selling them to magazines and still have enough time for my classes with Hilda. I called the managers of artists I liked and asked if I could shoot them. The rabbi always said, "Ask and ye shall receive." It made sense to me. After all, if you don't ask, what's the likelihood of getting what you want? When someone says "yes" to me, I do my best to make sure my actions provide benefits for them as well me. I'd show the artists their pictures then take them around to the magazines on my bicycle (which I still ride everywhere, no matter what the weather). Even if they didn't buy them, they'd hire me to shoot something for them. I still didn't think I was a professional photographer. I thought I was using the camera as a passport. It was my way into people's lives, into places that I otherwise might never see. Though I photographed people other than musicians, they were the dominant subject matter because it felt like I was simply hanging out with friends, maybe family.

Music and photography have made me feel whole most of my life. This combination always seemed fated. In 1982, I was in Nassau to photograph three artists: Robert Palmer, Marianne Faithfull, and Joe Cocker. Robert lived on the island. When I entered his home, he had a rhythm track playing which I recognized as James Brown's. He wanted to leave it on because he was looking for a melody. After doing some pictures, I suggested inviting Joe Cocker over, maybe

Wheeling and Dealing, 1975

Will Powers, 1984

he'd have a melody. Joe came over. We had a few drinks, made some pictures, and Joe improvised to the track. He left. Palmer said, "No, that wasn't it." I suggested asking Marianne to come over, maybe she'd have something. Over comes Marianne. More drinks, more pictures, some singing. She leaves. He says, "No, that wasn't it."

By now I've had enough drinks to give me the courage to suggest something I'd wanted to do for some time. I gave a "self-confidence" tape to Robert and asked if we could put it over the rhythm track. I'd had this idea about music having the power to instill positive or negative thinking. I knew lyrics affected me, even if I couldn't hear them clearly or understand them. I'm not a masterful songwriter or a great singer. The best I have to offer is my ideas. I wanted to make a record people could dance to and laugh with, and which, hopefully, might make them feel it was possible to make their dreams reality. Robert loved it and called Chris Blackwell, the owner of Island Records. He came by, listened, and wanted to put it out as an EP immediately.

I pleaded with him for the opportunity to make an album. I told him my ideas about self-help comedy set to dance music. Blackwell is a gambler and lucky for me, he decided to take a chance and let me do one song. I went to London where Sting helped me make the first track, "Adventures in Success." After Black-well heard it, he agreed to an album deal. I worked on the rest of the tracks with musicians who believed in my talent and lent theirs out of friendship—Sting, Steve Winwood, Todd Rundgren, and Nile Rogers.

Right before the release of the album, Andy Cavaliere, my best friend, died of a heart attack. Something changed inside me. I felt scared and confused. The record received immediate airplay as well as letters declaring how Will Powers had changed listeners' lives for the better. Some looked to Will as their new guru. Others accused Will of being "Disco est." But as much as I knew what I was trying to do, after Andy died I no longer felt clear about who I was, much less who "Will" was. I decided to put Will Powers to sleep and went back to making pictures.

Over the next ten years I photographed musicians, actors, writers, directors, politicians, sports stars, and businessmen as well as people all over the world in their everyday lives. No matter who I shoot or where I shoot, music always plays in the background. My cassette player is an indispensable piece of photo equipment. And now with camera in hand, I again feel clear about who I am— I'm "Lynnie" searching for the moment which can be shared with others because I've gotten it on film. For me, photographs and music are timeless reminders of the only thing that's real...love.

A Wop Bop Alu Bop A Wop Bam Boom!

strange

Strange angels is what I call musicians who behave in ways I wouldn't attempt to predict. Their actions are bizarre. Their choices have no rational explanation. They're simply inscrutable people. More often than not, these artists are the innovators, the originals. I've come to believe that musical genius only exists in people who are psychologically imbalanced.

angels

If you hang around with Bob Dylan long enough, someone is bound to come up and ask him if he is God, or tell him why they are sure he is God, or ask if he can he help them to find God. At moments like those I'm really happy I was born me and not him.

The odd part of being around him is that every once in a while he says something or does something which makes you think,

"Oh my God, it's Bob Dylan."

He told me to get out of his cab, he didn't want to drive "no assassins." I explained I was a photographer and the expression "to shoot" meant to take a picture. He took me to my destination.

I had been to this studio before and knew that the elevator door opened up right into the control room. As I rode the elevator and watched the lights mark each floor I knew that I had to make a very important decision. Was I a photographer or a fan? Did I come there to make the most of my time by creating a portrait, or did I

When I began making images of well-known people, I never felt intimidated. I thought of them as my subjects and all I really cared about was being able to make an image that would capture what I saw in them. But I never really experienced what it means to be a professional photographer until I got a call late one night in 1976 to come down to Secret Sound Studio to photograph Bob Dylan and Bette Midler. I grabbed my cameras and hopped in a cab. I was so excited I started talking to myself, saying over and over, "I'm going to shoot Dylan, Bob Dylan!" The driver heard me and pulled over.

come there to meet Bob Dylan? By the time the door opened I had chosen to be the best photographer I could be. There he was staring me right in the face. I walked right up to him, because I knew that even though I was invited, it was up to him if I'd get a shot. I stuck out my hand and introduced myself. "Hi, I'm Lynn Goldsmith and I'd like to make some pictures." He said, "Well that's not necessary, I have a photographer." I said, "With two photographers, you get two points of view!" He said, "I get your point of view." I said, "Then I can shoot, right?" He smiled and nodded yes.

bob dylan, new york 1976

7 years later...

Bob wore this sheepskin hat that I knew had covered his head for more than just a winter. When I announced my birthday was coming in a week, he asked me what I wanted. I told him, "Your hat." He responded, "No, not the hat. What else do you want?" I replied, "I only want the hat. I don't want anything else." I was startled by him offering me a present. I didn't really care if he gave me the hat or not. I didn't hear from him on my birthday, but a few weeks later the phone rang. He said, "Come on over, I got your birthday present." I was surprised he remembered my birthday, and somewhat shocked that he had a gift for me. When he presented me with the hat, he smiled warmly. I walked over to the mirror, put it on, and said, "This is not the hat." He looked surprised. I don't know why I said that. It was the hat. I think I got scared. I couldn't believe he gave me the one thing he told me he would not give up. I didn't want to be too close to him. It felt dangerous. That was not the last time I did something off-putting. As a matter of fact, I have always made sure that if there's even the slightest possibility of either of us feeling a romantic twinge, I do something to make him want to stay far away from me for a while, if not forever. I need a psychological screen between him and me. It's instinct.

bob dylan, new york 1983

kill

The session was scheduled to take place at his home in Malibu. I hired two assistants who were real Miles Davis fans and a hair and makeup person because Mr. Davis said he would not shoot without one. When we arrived I asked the assistants to wait in the car until I found the best place to set up. I rang the front doorbell. There was no answer. I walked around to the back of the house. Seeing him, I yelled, "Hi." He smiled and walked toward me. I stuck out my hand and introduced myself. His amazingly penetrating eyes looked warmly into mine. We talked a little bit about the beautiful weather. I sensed he had no idea who I was or why I was there, so I let him know I was the photographer who was scheduled to photograph him. He nodded and told me to follow him onto a terrace overlooking the ocean. There were four people having lunch. He said, "I'd like you to meet my fiance." Having photographed many talented musicians with great senses of humor, I thought it was very funny he had chosen to introduce me as his fiance. I threw my arms around him and said, "Why Miles, I didn't know you felt that way about me!"

Immediately, I knew two things: first, I made big mistake touching him; second, he was not introducing me as his fiance, he was introducing me to his fiance! Great way to start with a man you've always heard is difficult. I decided to call him Mr. Davis and apologized for making a stupid joke. Then, right to business. I asked him where he would like to be photographed. He pointed to the beach a hundred yards down a cliff. We had quite a bit of heavy equipment to carry, but it looked like a beautiful spot so I had the assistants take it all down to set up while I met with Mr. Davis on what he would wear. He asked me to watch a video of a photo shoot he'd done recently and to pick an outfit from it. Of course I didn't want to pick anything from a photo shoot he had just done, but it seemed best not to argue. "How about the black outfit?" He glared at me and said, "Why would I want to wear anything I already wore in a photograph?" I controlled myself. I just kept thinking, "This is Miles Davis; he is a genius." I asked again what he'd like to wear. He told me to go upstairs into his closet and pick something out. He also told me to

i thought i was going to him

go through his drawers. I said in disbelief, "You want me to go through your drawers?" He said harshly, "Don't you hear me?" I smiled nervously and went upstairs.

I selected an outfit with the aid of his publicist, who by this time was feeling sorry for me. As I came down the stairs with clothes in hand he said, "There is one outfit in my closet that I hate more than anything." I said, "Let me guess." He barked, "Where are you going to take this picture?" I said, "On the beach, where you told me." He said, "I never told you that. I will not shoot there." I held my hands together tightly because I wanted to hit him and said sweetly, "Where would you like to be photographed?" He pointed to the terrace. I suggested he pick out what he wanted to wear so I could help the assistants bring all the equipment back up from the beach. He agreed. I asked him if he wanted the hair and makeup person to go with him. He looked at me with what I now thought were the meanest eyes in the world and asked why I brought a hair and makeup person. I explained I was told he would not shoot unless I did. He walked off. My assistants and I got everything into place and made Polaroids of the shot. Miles came down and I showed them to him. He nodded and stepped into the spot, only he was about six inches too far to the right and part of a concrete sculpture was in the background. I didn't want it as part of the composition and asked him to move over six inches. I showed him the Polaroid again to make sure he understood why. In a very low voice he said, "Move it." In dis-

belief I replied, "What?" He repeated, "Move it." He wanted us to move the sculpture instead of him moving six inches. I thought I was going to kill him. My assistant saw that I was about to let loose; he grabbed my arm and said, "Lynn, we'll move it." I said through my teeth, "Don't you dare." He held my arm tightly and said, "You want the shot? We'll move it." I swallowed hard. I could not believe I had controlled myself to this point. I felt humiliated to have taken so much abuse. I asked Mr. Davis if we could get his horn for the shot. He used those killer eyes to say no. Physically I was ready to make pictures, but mentally I was a mess. I put on some Bulgarian folk music to cool myself out. He told me to "take off that white music." That was it. I didn't care anymore. I had thought of Miles Davis as a genius who went beyond color, especially when it came to music. I said in a very controlled sweet, soft voice, "You really are a bastard." For a split second all time stopped. Then he smiled at me. I smiled back and began shooting. He was giving to the camera. I still didn't like him and I was angry with myself for bothering to make pictures of such a jerk. Then he told his son to bring his horn. He lifted it to the blue sky and when the first sounds flowed out, I swear to God I thought I was in the presence of the Spirit. All of my hatred disappeared. I knew I would go through anything to be experiencing what I was right then. It's horrifying to think you can forgive a person completely just because of what they are capable of expressing musically. When I think of Miles Davis, I feel like one of the lucky ones who got to see Gabriel play his horn.

I feel like one of the lucky ones who got to see Gabriel play his horn.

I was in Boston on the road with the Jackson's Victory tour. I went to Michael's room around sunset and found him alone reading fairy tales. I asked if he wanted to make photographs in the magic light. He wanted to know what magic light was so he followed me to the hotel roof. While I was shooting he took off his shirt. It surprised me. Until that moment he had been an innocent child in my eyes.

I saw there was a **man** there too.

I was doing a cover shoot for <u>Life</u> magazine. Disney
World closed Epcot Center to the public so Michael would
not be disturbed. They treated him as if he was Mickey
Mouse reincarnated. Michael was over three hours late
and I was getting mad. His manager, Frank DeLio, told
me Michael was out doing his door-to-door work as a
Jehovah's Witness. I thought, "What a great excuse. How
can you get upset with someone who is trying to serve
God?" But how could Michael not think about all the people waiting for us to get our photography done so that they
could go back to work, or the visitors who might never
again have the opportunity to experience "the world of
make-believe?" The moment he arrived, he looked at me
and said in his little voice. "Lynn, you are so beautiful." All
my anger melted. He just smiled and I was a goner.

I was doing my James Brown moves and finally he joined me. I got to dance with Michael in the Tunnel of Light.

I first met him in 1974 in Zaire, Africa, at a press conference for the "Rumble in the Jungle" between George Foreman and Muhammad Ali. Ali was going on about how the white man took the black man's true names away, took his true dress away, and then he pointed at me and said, "The white man will send a white woman photographer before they would send a black photographer." James Brown jumped up and said, **"Wait a minute, the white man buys my records!"** I got to know him because he was there to play a music festival. We left Zaire on the same plane, which was delayed for five hours because Mr. Brown was fighting with the airport personnel about his equipment going with us. They said it made the plane too heavy. He didn't care. He said his equipment went with him. I don't know how he won but he did. ■ The second time we met was in Nassau eight years later. He walked out of his bungalow with pink sponge rollers in his hair. Reverend Al Sharpton and a bodyguard walked close behind. Mr. Brown told me I had to be searched before I could go inside his bungalow. I stood there in disbelief. There we were in the sunny Bahamas, I had been brought in by his record label, he remembered me from Zaire, and to my amazement, he was concerned that I might be carrying a weapon. I made a joke about coming there to shoot him. He didn't think it was funny. It was clear there would be no picture taking without a search so I agreed. His bodyguard did a kind of airport check on me and my camera bag. I guess when you are "The Godfather of Soul," you get to call the shots.

She liked

going around

with

no

clothes

on

because

she

was

just more

comfortable

that

way.

I had an assignment from <u>Newsweek</u> to photograph Prince and I was really excited because I thought he was a great artist. I was sure he would be incredible in front of the camera and that I would become his new best friend. He came in and stood on my white seamless for about sixty seconds. I shot less than a roll of film. He walked off the set and went into the dressing room. I waited five minutes and then used the intercom to ask if everything was all right. There was no reply. I waited another five minutes and then knocked on the door. Still no reply. I told him that if I didn't hear anything in the next five minutes, if he didn't come out, then I was coming in. I waited. No reply. I opened the door and he was just sitting on the edge of the couch. I sat on the other edge. After a few moments I said "Is it my breath?" No response. "Ok, is it body odor, do I have B.O.?" No response. "My clothes, you hate my clothes, right?" Nothing. Not a crack of a smile, not even a sideways glance in my direction. We sat in silence for a minute which for me was an eternity. Suddenly I was overcome with an unexpected emotional pain. Tears rolled down my eyes as I quietly told him, "I feel like I'm to blame because I can't get through to you." I wiped my eyes and left the room. Twelve years later he booked me for a photo session in L.A. I didn't know if it was really going to happen until about two hours before he arrived. As soon as I started shooting, he began working for the camera and was so good that all my "yeah, yeah's" came bursting out. The makeup artist who had worked with him for years came over and suggested I not make any sounds. The next thing I knew he was gone.

prince is a mystery to me

Style

In the late seventies and early eighties magazines and record companies refused to pay for professional styling, hair, or makeup, so I did it myself or got friends who did that kind of work to help me for very little money. I paid the added costs because I wanted to make musicians look their best. Often it was a struggle to get them to change their clothing or wear makeup because they thought it meant they had less integrity as artists. In order to get Chrissie Hynde to wear makeup, I showed her pictures of Patti Smith. I thought I'd have a better chance of convincing her if she saw someone she respected in makeup. If an artist was particularly difficult, I'd pull out a picture of Dylan and tell them he wore makeup. It was a lie, but I knew once they saw his picture, they'd give in and let me work to the best of my ability. When MTV came along the record companies suddenly wanted to have hair, makeup, and styling. Today most artists won't do a photo session without it. Everyone in the business is now aware of how visual image is a crucial part of the success or failure of the record. I'm happy that it's no longer a battle to get budgets for help, but it makes me sad to think that there are musicians out there whose music won't get the attention it deserves because they trusted the wrong visual people.

The first photo session was in L.A. I thought she had a horrible hairdo and terrible clothes. She liked working with me and agreed to do a session in my New York studio. This time I had a hair and makeup person. She cut off Pat's hair and completely changed her makeup. We put her in clothes rented from Norma Kamali. The session was done at my expense. I liked Pat, thought she was my new friend, and was excited about giving her a fresh image because there were so few women in music at that time. We placed the photographs in <u>Newsweek,</u> <u>People,</u> <u>Vogue,</u> and other magazines. Selling those pictures at editorial rates does not make one rich. In fact, it barely paid for the shooting. I had hoped she would appreciate what my team had done for her but Pat became very popular and I never heard from her again.

Devo arrived at my studio in ordinary street clothes except for Mark. **He was wearing a metallic racing bicycle seat on his head. He explained, "I'm really very shy** and when I see a girl I like, I bend down on one knee and ask them if they'd like to go for a ride on my bicycle. Besides that, it's raining outside."

debbie

had been a cosmetologist and knew how to do hair and makeup. She took about an hour to work on herself. I watched in the mirror. After that session, I always tried to have professional hair and makeup people involved whenever possible because I saw how much better artists could look, even if they were beautiful to begin with.

This was taken before the Go-Go's first record was relea
lived. It was kind of like visiting a college sorority house.

sed. It was shot at Belinda's house where a few of them
They helped each other with hair, makeup, and clothes.

For the first time I saw someone I felt was truly

androgynous.

He walked into the studio in high-waisted green continental pants, gold chains, and a Las Vegas greaseball hairdo. I'd seen him perform the night before and he was pure rockabilly. I wanted to match his look to how I thought he sounded. He said he couldn't stay long because his plane was waiting on the runway. I told him to either tell the pilot to shut off the engines or he might as well leave because what I wanted to do would take some time. He stayed. We cut his hair, got him in some tight black jeans and cowboy boots, and just blasted his music. He seemed happy to meet people who thought of him the way we did. The next day his manager called and said Ricky had thrown out all his clothes and wanted to know where he should go shopping.

Cindy was sweet, but distant.

Before she would step in front of the camera, she'd always ask her brother, Ricky, for approval on how she looked. When he died I felt badly. I liked him and I also sensed how much Cindy would miss him for the rest of her life.

My first photo studio was in my apartment. Often during shoots, I'd pull clothes, jewelry hats, etc. from my closets. When I moved the studio out of my home, I made sure to fill the new makeup room closets with costumes, wigs, and assorted props. During the shoot I'd start pulling everything out to see what might inspire both me and the artist. It was the most fun to do with females because

I felt like I was twelve years old again, playing dress up with my girlfriends.

eurythmics, new york 1984

martika, new york 1989

When going on location. I'd bring a bag of props and hope the artists would find something that would make them pose in a way they never had before.

TRUST IS A MUST

I thought Daryl Hall was too pretty. I wanted to him to have a tough look. I asked him to wear my studded black leather jacket. It was too small for him, but I promised it would be a close-up and no one would ever see how silly the short arms looked. The jacket put him in a different mood so then he let me slick back his hair. When he looked in the mirror to check it out, a different person was looking back. I thought he had beautiful hands so I added the cigarette as a prop. Daryl trusted me and that allowed us to have fun making pictures.

JOE STRUMMER, NEW YORK 1984

VANILLA ICE, BOSTON 1991

CHRISSIE HYNDE, NEW YORK 1980

GRACE SLICK, LOS ANGELES 1989

LENNY KRAVITZ, LOS ANGELES 1991

DARYL HALL, NEW YORK 1976

TINA WEYMOUTH, NEW YORK 1980

INXS, LOS ANGELES 1987

YA KID K, NEW YORK 1990

GRACE JONES, NASSAU 1982

BRET MICHAELS OF POISON, LOS ANGELES 1993

CATHY DENNIS, NEW YORK 1990

BRYAN ADAMS, NEW YORK 1984

2 to 20

The publicist tells me I'll get anywhere from two to twenty minutes to make a picture. They explain how the artist hates having his picture taken, or how hectic her schedule is. No matter how much homework I do to find out about the person I'm shooting, the time pressure makes it hard for me to do my best work. To create a telling portrait of someone you've never met is not an easy task, especially when you can't even have a conversation to establish rapport before you start shooting. Imagine being told you have two minutes to shoot and having a publicist stand there counting off the time. And you're trying to make a portrait that might be compared to another where the photographer could have had an entire day to shoot with a hairdresser, make-up artist and stylist. One part of me feels angry and humiliated. One part tells me to just concentrate and do the best I can. Making pictures this way is like sex with no foreplay, "slam, bang, thank you ma'am." Why do I put up with this?

1) There's a slim possibility I might make an image I'm happy about.

2) I want to meet the person.

3) I might make a connection for the future when I'll be able to create better conditions.

4) I'd rather make pictures than not make pictures.

The record company publicist tells me "Rick is the lead—make sure you keep him up front. Try to do something that gives off some kind of vibe as to who they are and get at least three group setups as well as individual shots. We don't have enough money in the budget for you to have an assistant. Oh yeah, you can have them for one hour." This is when I wonder why I'm making pictures. Five people I've never met before, who range in size from 5'4" to 6'2", together in pictures with no hair, no makeup, no styling, no help.

I had a couple vo
every

dkas and
thing turned out ok.

I can't imagine how individuals as shy as she is can get on a stage in front of people and sing. It makes me think that **if someone has a true musical gift, they have no other choice than to share it.**

I was told there'd be twenty minutes
to shoot before her show at Radio City,

so I turned the ladies bath-room into a photo studio.

Paula was extremely sweet and knew
how to "work" the camera. Her hair
and makeup were done for the stage
show, not for a photo session. I kept
thinking about the pictures I might
have made with my own hair, makeup, and stylists.

When looking at some of these images, I laugh because I know the viewer will never be aware they were shot under immense pressure in a toilet.

I drove with a twelve-foot roll of seamless paper hanging out my car window for six hours to get to Roger Daltrey at some remote seaside locale. When I arrived, he said he didn't feel like being photographed. He wanted to go for a walk. I told him I'd follow behind and maybe along the way he'd let me know if it was all right to take pictures. Slowly, he walked down toward the water. Since he was fully clothed, I thought he'd stop at the shoreline, but he just kept walking. I followed, holding the cameras over my head. Once his mouth was covered with water I said,

"It's OK to shoot now, right?"

He had no time to answer.

What if

they hadn't been successful?
Who would they be married to?
Where would they live?
What cars would they drive?
Where would they shop?

Imagine

this guy comes here from Russia, gets himself a great look-ing girlfriend who can really sing, and puts a band together. Ain't that the American dream?

I had two girlfriends who claimed to be deeply in love with him. Each of them thought, of course, that he felt the same way about her. The unfortunate part was hearing it from both of them simultaneously. **I thought his surname** Years later, I was asked to photograph him because of his fight to save Walden Woods. I drove four hours to get there and when I arrived I was told I'd have twenty minutes. This plus my recalling how both my friends ended up with broken hearts, didn't make me too excited about the job. I set up by Walden Pond and waited for him to arrive. He got out of his limo and greeted me as if we'd met before. I asked him to walk back and forth by the pond. He looked unhappy. I asked if anything was wrong and he sweetly explained how this fight was not about the pond but the woods! I felt pretty stupid. We went up to the woods to shoot. My time was short, but long enough for me to I understand why my girlfriends had been so enchanted.

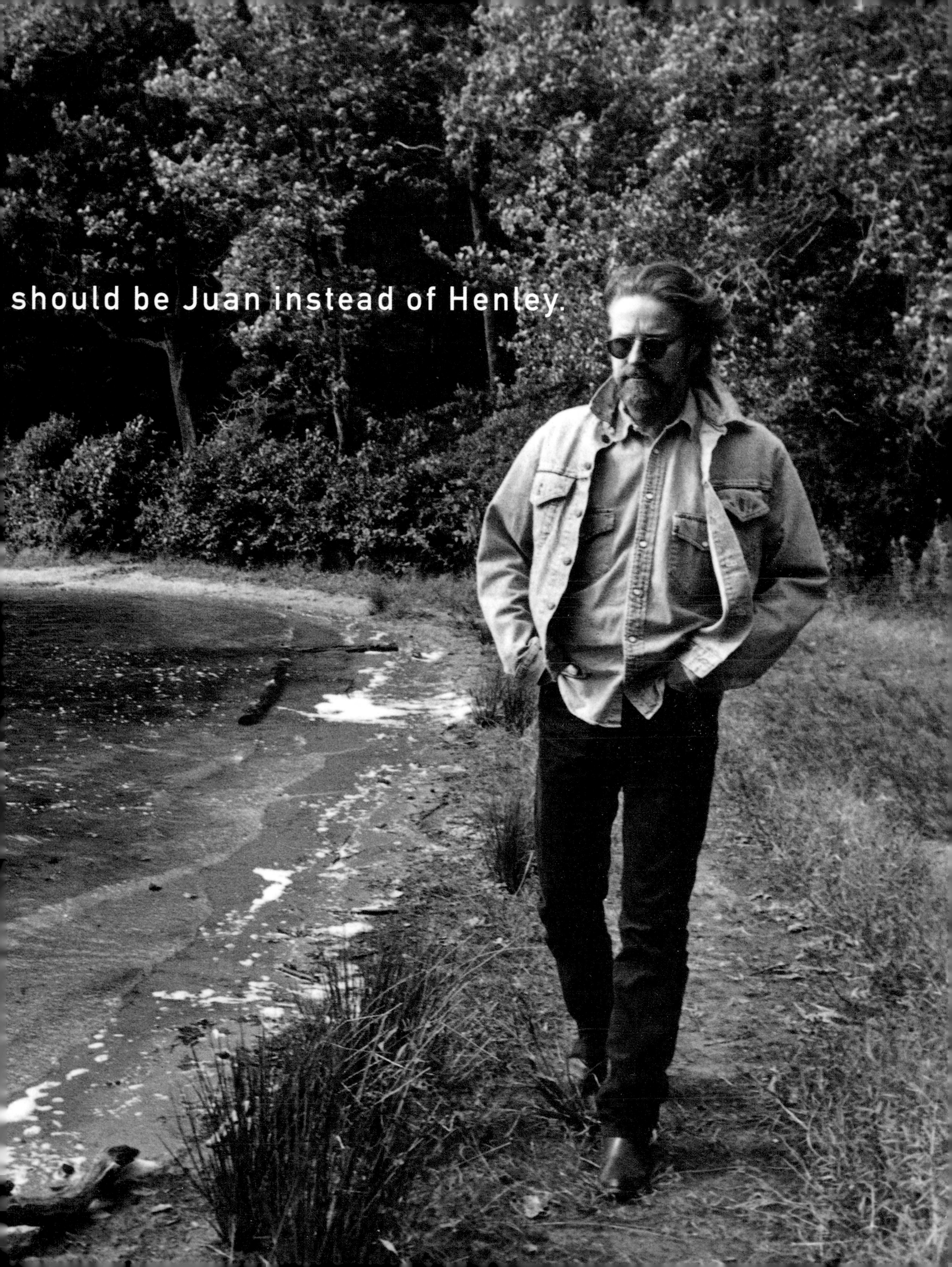

should be Juan instead of Henley.

I had two minutes with her at the 1993 Presidential Inauguration.

Though I've never had a lesbian experience, I was physically attracted to her.

I spoke about this with a couple of my heterosexual girlfriends
and they confided feeling the same way about her.

robbie robertson, los angeles 1987

Pictures are the last thing they want to do.

karl wallinger of world party, england 1987

tom petty. los angeles 1980

BLIND MELON, NEW YORK 1993

DWIGHT YOAKAM, LOS ANGELES 1993

STEELY DAN, NEW YORK 1993

YOKO ONO & SEAN LENNON, LONDON 1990

KENNY G, NEW YORK 1987

THESE KINDS OF JOBS REQUIRE A LOT OF PHYSICAL EFFORT.

I flew to Minneapolis to shoot Genesis for <u>Stern</u> magazine. You have to bring lighting equipment and backdrops, rent a car, find the venue, get security to let you unload, and that's just for starters. Warned at least a dozen times that I would have no more than twenty minutes to shoot, I tried to set up in their small dressing room as quickly as possible. I'd never met them. When they came in they were nice enough, but I was on the clock and they were not dressed to be in pictures together. I asked them to change quickly into something gray or black. I powdered each one and told them where to stand on the seamless.

In an effort to establish some nonverbal connection, I blasted <u>James Brown Live from Japan</u> on my tape machine. The publicist kept telling me how much time was left and finally to pack up and get out as quickly as possible. "No, you can't have seats to watch the show." We loaded the equipment, headed back to airport, returned the car, and waited three hours for our flight. Back home everyone thought it was really great that I shot Genesis.

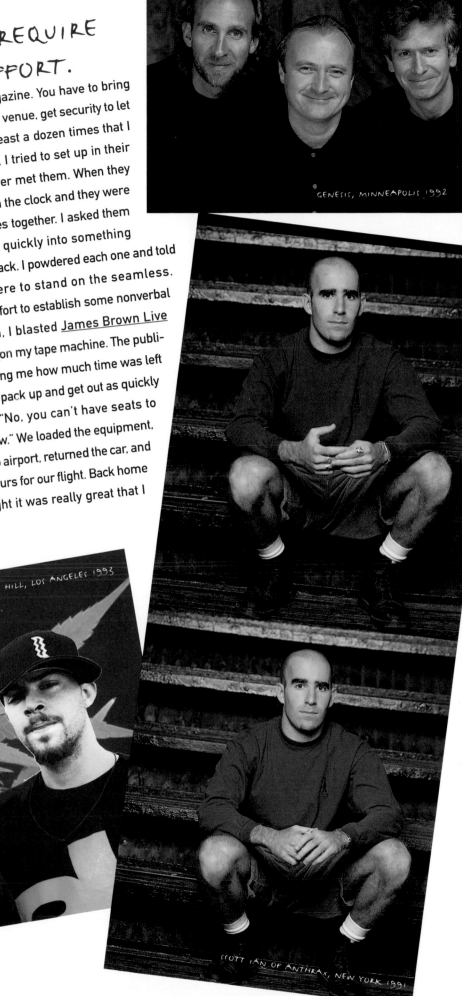

GENESIS, MINNEAPOLIS, 1992

RUSSELL SIMMONS, NEW YORK, 1993

CYPRESS HILL, LOS ANGELES, 1993

SCOTT IAN OF ANTHRAX, NEW YORK, 1991

When a shoot is going well, I unconsciously say "yeah, yeah, yeah" over and over in an excited tone of voice. Often, my subject, or anyone else who's there, thinks I'm coming on or getting off. But I'm just naturally expressing how everything feels perfect in that moment: the subject, the expression, the light, the hair, the makeup. Yeah. It's sex, but it's purely mental sex. I got married to photography because it feels so good.

better than sex

Patti Smith came home from London and told me
she'd found an angel named Paul. He played bass
with a band she saw in some tiny underground club.
She was in the middle of reading me a letter he
wrote (girlfriends do that!) when he called. Paul said
things were hard for the group. They had no money.
After that conversation, she picked up the phone
and called Walter Yetnikoff, the president of CBS
Records, at his home. She told him he ought to sign
this band she'd heard. The rest is Clash history.

I showed him my pictures of his dad.
While we were shooting he kept asking me something over and over.
Because of his accent, I didn't understand what he was saying. I'd smile
and continue shooting. When he left,
my assistant told me Ziggy wanted to
know if I'd slept with his father.

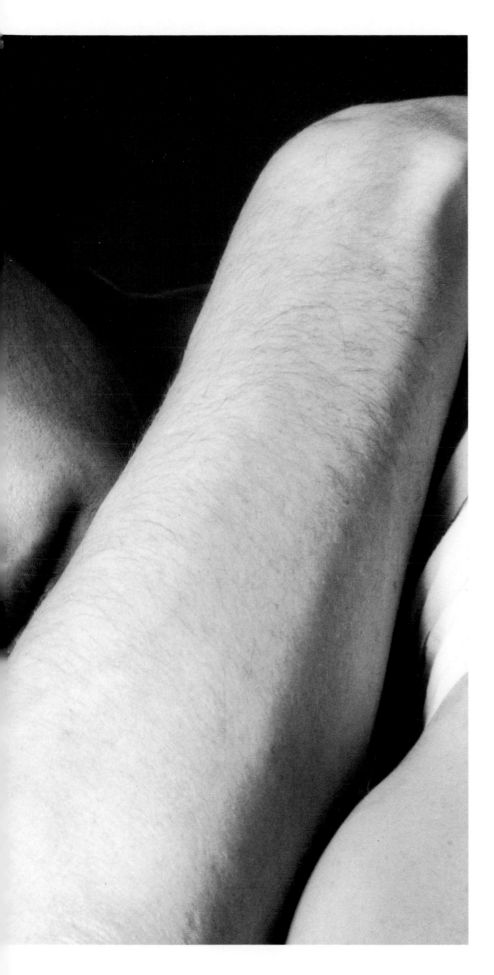

The Boomtown Rats had come to America for the first time. The buzz in the business was they could be "the next big thing." I liked that Bob Geldof, the lead singer/songwriter, had been a rock writer who faced up to the fact that

he really wanted to be a rock star and went for it.

During the session Bob asked if I could help his girlfriend, Paula Yates, get some photographs of rock stars in their underwear for a book she was doing. I couldn't believe it. I said if I had pictures like that, why would I want them published? He said that it was part of what rock and roll is all about. I didn't really understand but I knew he was an extremely convincing, well-intentioned guy who could find a rationale for any goal he aimed for.

For me, Tom's work expressed appreciation for the complexity of our human reality. **It made me feel glad I was me.** I wanted to be friends with him. It never happened. I think that if I'd been a guy, we might have known each other better. **Sometimes being female really gets in the way** because I don't pursue a relationship for fear it will be presumed that I want something romantic to happen.

Even though all of them were completely naked, I never actually saw Grand Funk's private parts. They weren't hiding anything— it's just that I was concentrating really hard on the composition of the photograph. People would ask me who had the biggest penis. No one believed I didn't take close notice

of that particular part of their anatomy.

HOLD IT!

The moment I click on an image which feels like I hit the center of a bull's eye, a sound comes out of me that's beyond "yeah, yeah, yeah." It's difficult to describe. It's kind of a squeal. Once a session was filmed when it happened and I was mortified when I heard it. I've tried not to let it come out, but it does. The nice part about the sound is that everyone working with me knows we got the shot.

RICK NIELSEN, NEW YORK, 1980

SIOUXSIE SIOUX, NEW YORK 1980

TANYA TUCKER, LOS ANGELES 1979

SUSANNA HOFFS, MALIBU 1989

HEAVY D, NEW YORK 1991

ROBERT PALMER, NASSAU 1982

on the road

People who 've never been on the road with a rock group think there's some mysterious glamour to it. Here's how it is: You get on a plane or a bus and travel to a hotel or venue. If you arrive at a hotel, you try to get a little sleep before leaving for the venue. At the venue there's a lot of waiting around and bad food. The show lasts for a few hours and then you're back on the bus trying to sleep in a cramped seat, rolling on to the next place that looks exactly like the last place because you never really saw any place anyway. You try to get time with the artist to make some special 'set-up' photographs, but it rarely happens. For the most part, all anyone talks about is the "star." Life revolves around gossip, as if nothing of any importance is going on in the world. The only good part is that for a short time there's a sense of family bond. But at the end of the road you go your own way.

Rolling Stone sent me to photograph the Stones in London. Their publicist, Alvinia Bridges, told me I had to shoot from the Queen's Box, about a mile from the stage. I hadn't brought long enough lenses for that and I explained that I needed to shoot from the front of the stage. She went to the head publicist Paul Wasserman. Then I saw them huddling with Bill Graham, the legendary promoter. He was shaking his head no. Alvinia told me I had to leave the stage area and go back to the Queen's Box. They might as well have told me to go back to New York. At that moment it started pouring rain. I ran for cover into Black Uhuru's backstage area; they were opening for the Stones. Standing there, tired, hungry, cold, wet, and angry, I wondered how I could get out of there and on the first plane back home. Suddenly, I heard someone with an English accent say, "You don't look happy." I was so upset I refused to look up. I just said, "Right." He said, "Anything I can do?" I looked up and it was Mick! I explained what happened and he told me to come with him. We walked over to Alvinia. He simply said, "She's shooting from the stage." She smiled at him, but as soon as he walked away she looked at me angrily. She ran to tell Paul Wasserman, Paul told Bill Graham—it was easy to see they were not happy with me. But when Divine Providence makes sure you're going to get the shot, are you going to argue? Mick took me up on stage with him and put me on the side by the speakers.

The show started and I was happily shooting away when Bill Graham came over, grabbed my arm, and dragged me to the back of the stage behind a screen. Soon Mick noticed I wasn't where he put me and he comes over and asks me why I moved. The Stones are in the middle of a show! I'm stunned. I explain that Bill Graham moved me. Mick took my arm and put me in the spot I originally shot from. On the other side of the stage I could see Bill screaming and yelling. I knew that for the rest of his life Bill Graham would hold it against me.

That's Rock and Roll.

NEW YORK 1975

LOS ANGELES 1978

WITH LINDA RONSTADT, ARIZONA 1978

WITH JERRY HALL, LOS ANGELES 1978

ARIZONA 1978

MICK'S PARENTS,
LONDON 1982

WITH PETER TOSH, TEXAS 1978

WITH ANDY WARHOL, NEW YORK 1977

SYMPATHY FOR THE PHOTOGRAPHER

When the show is over you have to run to the cars which are going to the airport where a private jet is waiting to take off. I'm running as fast as I can when a huge security guard scoops me up off my feet. I'm showing my passes and pleading with him to put me down. Some of the crew run by, paying no attention. I'm going to miss the plane if he doesn't let me go. I start screaming, "I'm with them, put me down." He's laughing. Next thing I know Keith has come back for me. He nicely tells the guy to put me down. The idiot is in shock. A Rolling Stone is actually speaking to him. He asks me if he can borrow a pen so he can get Keith's autograph.

LOS ANGELES 1978

NEW YORK 1977

TEXAS 1978

WITH FAMILY, LONDON 1982

LONDON 1982

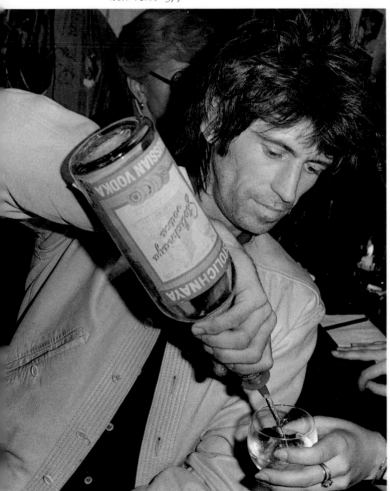

ARIZONA 1978

BILL WYMAN WITH FAMILY, LONDON 1982

LOS ANGELES 1978

RON WOOD, SAN FRANCISCO 1978

CHARLIE WATTS WITH SLY & ROBBIE, LONDON 1982

WITH STEVE McQUEEN, LOS ANGELES 1978

NEW YORK 1978

bob marley, italy 1980

I went on tour with the Wailers in Italy. I couldn't understand their Jamaican accent so I didn't talk much and they didn't talk to me. This was good and bad. The good part was that they never minded having me in the room when they were discussing something private because they knew it was a foreign language to me. The bad part was that I felt lonely. One day on the bus, the guy sitting in front of me was toking on a huge spliff. I asked if I could have some, thinking this might begin a friendship. He screamed at me something I didn't understand. I had no idea that for Rastafarians smoking was a religious act and that you don't share it. Bob was sitting across from me reading the Bible. Without saying a word, he handed me his spliff to smoke.

From that moment on I had the official ok.

yanni. athens 1993

He paid for us to be able to shoot at the Parthenon in Athens after closing time. We shot until dark. Yanni returned to his hotel but my assistant and I stayed and watched the full moon come up over this ancient building. One of the real gifts of my job is to be able to experience things that most people never have the opportunity to see or do.

There are sessions where the experience leaves me feeling I had a bad dream. In some cases, it's because the artist I'm photographing is a surprising disappointment to me as a human being. In other cases, the artist might be more wonderful than what I expected, but something happens which stops me from shooting as much as I wanted. Sometimes I experience making pictures as a job I despise because of what I have to go through to get the shot. But these are just moments. There are always better moments.

photo nightmares

When she walked in the door, I was shocked. She was fat! I was more shocked when she insisted on taking her clothes off. I kept trying to get her to put them back on. The next day, when I spoke of her weight to her publicist, she explained Nina was pregnant. They hadn't told me because they wanted to keep it a secret!

If you flirt with
Chuck Berry
be prepared to
**put
out
or
get
out.**

When he walked in I thought he looked familiar. Not because he was Mr. Cat Scratch Fever, but from something in my past. While I was shooting it came up in conversation that we were from the same neighborhood in Detroit. I told him how when I was twelve years old, my girlfriend and I would spend hours teasing and spraying our hair, putting on pink lipstick and toreador pants, and then walk over to the Dairy Queen where we would act real sexy. We'd go up to some guy and say, "Wanna go to Boblo?" (To get there you had to take a boat and it was well known as a place that "fast" girls went.) The guys would always respond with an enthusiastic,

"Yeah!"

Then I'd say, "My mother told me to take a fairy!" My girlfriend and I would scream with laughter and run off. Well, one day there was this guy who I didn't run from fast enough and he shoved a Dairy Queen right in my face. Guess who!

I wanted to tell him how Springsteen used to play me Bo Diddley records and point out exactly what he lifted from them, but I didn't because the first thing he started talking about was how **the white musician stole all his licks and made all the money.**

We were shooting in Nassau on the beach. I thought, Let's all go into the ocean. I worked so hard convincing them to do it, I never thought about the danger of taking my camera and my powerful flash into the water.

I got the shot I wanted. I also got the shock of my life.

We played the music very loud. I danced with her as I shot to keep her moving. I'd try to follow whatever she did and shoot at the same time. She threw her head around from right to left, over and over. I would swing my head back at her. It was like we were speaking some secret language. This went on for a couple of hours, then she left. While shooting, I noticed she had a very thick neck. The next day I was in a lot of pain and had to go to the doctor. He put me in a neck brace which I wore for three weeks.

Now I know how Tina Turner developed those neck muscles.

Keith had a reputation

for showing up at places and having to be carried out of them. With this in mind, I decided to have the clothes changes on set instead of in the dressing room. I didn't want him to leave my sight. As I took pictures he changed shirts, assistants changed backgrounds, and the music blasted. Things were going really well. Though he drank a couple of bottles of whiskey and smoked some of the biggest joints I'd ever seen, he didn't appear the least bit drunk or stoned. Keith had brought his girlfriend, Patti Hansen, who had been watching it all. I asked her to be in some pictures with him. She seemed to float right into his arms. They held each other and started turning in a circle. My assistants and I followed them like a team. It felt as though we were all part of his dance. But something was wrong. I was seeing two Keiths and two Pattis. I excused myself and went into the bathroom. After about an hour, one of the assistants came into the bathroom and saw me lying on the floor. She closed the door and told Keith I was too shy to come out! The session was over. I never imagined that breathing the same air as him could be that dangerous. I never thought it would be me, not Keith Richards, who would pass out at the shoot.

patti hansen & keith richards, new york 1981

It surprised me how easily Ringo came on to the camera. He seemed to like having his picture taken, so I was having fun. He asked if he could wear my leather jacket. He put it on, we took a few shots, then he said he wanted to buy it. I told him it wasn't for sale. It was a gift from my friend, designer Michael Schmidt. He persisted. I explained again that it was a present and had sentimental value for me. It

He walked out.

wasn't for sale. I suggested Michael could make him one. He wanted that jacket right then and there. He offered to buy it and to give me his jacket. The atmosphere in the room became tense. Trying to lighten it, I joked that if he wanted it because of the chain-linked skull and crossbones on the back, I had a car in L.A. with skulls all over it and he could buy that! This didn't help. He wanted my jacket. I wanted to keep it.

The session was over.

I decided to get down on my knees and wave my

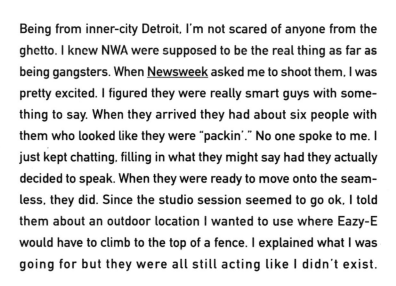

Being from inner-city Detroit, I'm not scared of anyone from the ghetto. I knew NWA were supposed to be the real thing as far as being gangsters. When <u>Newsweek</u> asked me to shoot them, I was pretty excited. I figured they were really smart guys with something to say. When they arrived they had about six people with them who looked like they were "packin'." No one spoke to me. I just kept chatting, filling in what they might say had they actually decided to speak. When they were ready to move onto the seamless, they did. Since the studio session seemed to go ok, I told them about an outdoor location I wanted to use where Eazy-E would have to climb to the top of a fence. I explained what I was going for but they were all still acting like I didn't exist.

arms up and down like I was worshipping them.

It worked. They all laughed and did as I asked from then on.

All he really wanted to do was stay home or walk his dogs.

neil young. two bunch palms 1994

I had tried to photograph Neil for ten years. I'd ask magazines to assign me, I'd ask the record label, I'd tell manage-
ment I'd work with whatever budget they had. The answer
was always "Neil doesn't want to do any pictures now." I
wanted him to be part of this book because his music had
been part of my life. But I gave up. After all the images for
the book were chosen, I wanted to get away from thinking
about it. I decided to take my mom to Two Bunch Palms, a
health spa in the California desert. Upon arriving, we went to
sign in for our massage, facials, mud bath, and assorted reju-
venation appointments. As I'm booking our times, the person behind the desk smiled and welcomed the person
standing behind me. I think she called him Mr. Boris. I felt a
strong presence. I turned around and it was Neil Young. I
couldn't believe it, I'd come here to get away from it all and
here is the person I wanted to shoot most, right behind me.
Two Bunch Palms is a place where people go to relax, and
since he was using a fake name, I really didn't feel comfortable acknowledging I knew who he was, much less that I
wanted to photograph him. The next three days were incredibly stressful. I'd go to the hot springs and five minutes later,
he'd come in and float around. I'd go to take a mud bath and
he'd be one curtain pull away. At meals, he'd sit with his wife
at a table I could have reached out and touched. I was crazy
with the urge to ask him to let me make pictures. Plus, the
room they were staying in once belonged to the gangster Al
Capone. All I could think about was what a great shot this
would be if he'd only give me five minutes. On our last day
there I saw him come out of his cabin with hair all slicked
back, wearing sunglasses and a long black robe with "Harley
Davidson" embroidered on the back. I've never seen him look
better. We were checking out. This was my last chance. I
couldn't stand it, I picked up my camera and took one shot,

teen idols

I always thought teen idols were a good thing, especially for us girls. They gave us the opportunity to love unconditionally. They gave us our own set of heroes, our own magazines to buy, our own styles, our own identities as teenagers. It was part of growing up. Some of us loved the greats like Chuck Berry, Jerry Lee Lewis, Elvis, or The Beatles, but our feelings were no different from the feelings of those who loved Fabian, David Cassidy, or New Kids On The Block. Bless them all. The beauty of loving someone at that age is the likelihood you'll love them forever.

We were walking down a beach in Hawaii at night. The stars were shining brighter than I'd ever seen. Neither of us were talking. I was thinking about how small we are in this universe. David broke the silence by saying,

"You know, Lynn, I'm a legend in my own time."

I wanted to tell him he was a legend in his own mind.

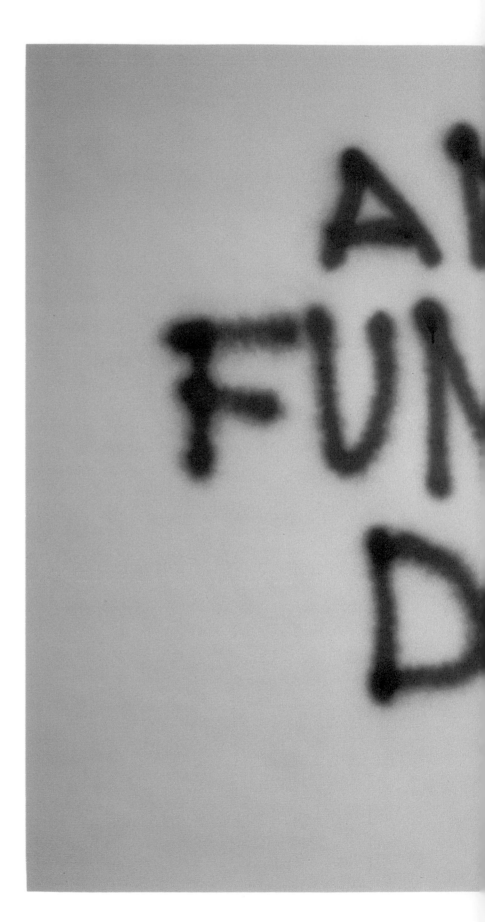

I gave him a spray can and asked him to write whatever came to mind.

Shaun, like most teen idols, wanted to be taken seriously. But unlike most, he didn't resent his success. He appreciated it.

leif garrett, los angeles 1980

Teen idols who resent being teen idols have a strong tendency to dislike their fans and end up doing drugs.

It was no surprise to find more than one generation visiting his grave. He was the prototype of our most beloved kind of star:

the doomed.

john wanted to be

I knew him as John Cougar, a teen pop
star who wanted respect from the music
industry. Few people took him seriously
as an artist. He was angry and frustrat-
ed. I think this made him dig deeper
inside himself. John did his absolute best
to create an identity out of language and
desire and, in my opinion, he succeeded.

bruce

I went to a concert in Florida and shot two rolls of film: one black and white, one color. I showed the color to RCA and they paid me $75 for all rights to them. I was happy because it paid for my concert ticket and my film and because

I knew Elvis would

women

The first time I met him was at a party INXS had in L.A.

have

I was staring at him thinking, this is the guy Elvis hung

been

out with, when a beautiful model type walked by and I

giving

saw her stick a black lace bra in his pocket. He

him

noticed, but just kept talking to the people he was with

their

as if she were not even there. She was trying every-

under-

thing to get his attention. He left by himself soon after-

wear

ward. A year later he came to my studio for a photo

for

session and I understood why he was so cool.

years

They were one of the first acts whose video on MTV made the record sell. It was all about the way they looked.

Little girls went crazy. Some big ones did too.

This picture was taken at the start of their career in the U.S. before they had hair, makeup, or styling.

Good people

Sometimes the people I photograph thank me and everyone else who helped at the shoot. Sometimes they send a note of gratitude or flowers. Some people make you feel they think about more than just themselves. They are truly good people. And they make it all worthwhile.

linda ronstadt, texas 1978

Their first album came out and zoomed to the top of the charts. Everybody was talking about them. They had a reputation for behaving like wild animals. I was warned they might walk in and stay only a few minutes, and that everything in my studio should be tied down. They were going to be a nightmare. I looked into who the Beastie Boys are and discovered they come from good homes with strong educational backgrounds. I thought their rebellious actions had to be some kind of act, but just to make sure that they'd stay and do what I wanted, I booked a beautiful model who was prepared to do nudes. When they came in I told them about my idea of shooting them playing strip poker and then introduced the model, who was wearing black lingerie. They became very quiet, very shy. Each of them acted their part perfectly and was respectful to the model. I loved working with them.

I think they are three really smart guys with a vision.

Blondie had just released their first record when we met. Chris and Debbie seemed the ideal couple. He was the brains and she was the beauty. They lived in a small cluttered apartment and appeared to be inseparable. Both were music fans. They wanted me to tell them stories about the Stones, Patti Smith, James Brown, etc. I told them one day they'd be really successful and then they wouldn't be so impressed that I knew these people. Blondie had lots of hits. Chris and Debbie got to be friends with many of the people they admired. They also got heavily into drugs and eventually broke up.

I wish I could turn the clock back and keep the innocent ones innocent forever.

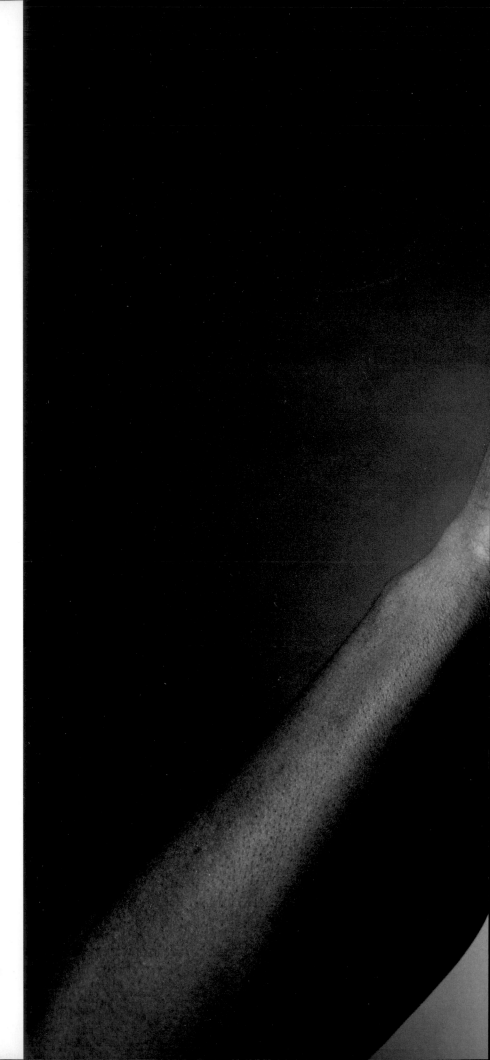

He's a

showman,

a

pioneer,

a

survivor,

and a

gentleman.

I met U2 at the beginning of their career. They were the first band I saw pray together before going on stage. I'd had a few conversations about God with Bono. He knew of my spiritual teacher, Hilda. **To my surprise, one of the first people I heard from when Andy Cavaliere died was Bono.** The doorbell rang and there he was. Because of my distraught state I don't remember much except Bono getting down on his knees, taking my hand, and leading me in prayer.

I met David in 1969.

I loved his smile. He was a warm person and I had a real crush on him. Years later he started a record label and I went to see him to show him my work. He was already extremely successful but he still seemed humble. I told someone about my crush on him and they informed me that he really wasn't interested in women. Not long after that I heard he was going with Cher. I was disappointed. I thought Cher was smart and funny and independent and that I would never have a chance with him. The years passed and David Geffen got more and more powerful. I shot him in his Malibu home, and found him to be one of the most considerate individuals I've ever worked with, both to my assistants and to me. He shows respect to other people simply because they are people. Whenever I'm photographing someone who thinks he or she is so almighty that it gives them the right to behave badly toward me or my crew, I think about David. He's got the kind of success that matters most, a good heart and a generous spirit.

pee

In the early days of my career, my apartment was also my studio. Bruce Springsteen was my boyfriend. I didn't want anyone to know about it because I didn't want to be known as his or anybody else's girlfriend. I wanted to be known for my work. I was nuts. Who cares what other people think! Back then, I did. Bruce knew I had a session with Randy Newman and wanted to meet him. I absolutely refused. I planned the session for when I thought Bruce wouldn't be around. He didn't leave for the recording studio at the usual time and he was there when Randy arrived. I made Bruce stay in another room. He made me promise to photograph Randy in his jacket. Randy put it on for a few shots but wanted to take it off. He said it smelled.

yew

We shot
in his
apartment.
Luther
makes you
feel like
his home
is your
home.

Meatloaf is chivalrous.

Meatloaf was the only person at the
MUSE concert who went to Bruce's
dressing room and told him he was
a jerk to do what he did to me.

During one of our shoots, I knocked over his trumpet. I

freaked. Some musicians don't want you to touch their "axe,"

much less drop it on a concrete floor!

what
did he
do?

He said, "Oh, don't worry,

it's only a piece of metal."

He's the kind of guy I could see myself married to. He's into spirituality in an
involved in his work that he would leave me alone to do mine. And we could

earthy way and has a sense of humor to match his intelligence. He's so
go travel the world together. Too bad he never showed any interest in me.

I had photographed Michelle before. I thought she was not only one of the sweetest people I'd ever worked with, but one of the most beautiful. This time I was going to photograph her with her teenage daughter, Chynna. During the session we ordered lunch. The sandwich Chynna ordered came and had mayonnaise or something on it that she didn't want. She threw a fit. Her mom calmed her down. I thought, Michelle, why don't you just slap her! As the years passed by I got to know Chynna. She was just as kind and considerate as her mom.

I had forgotten what it's like to be fourteen.

Photography has brought me so much. Best of all, close personal relationships.

Friends & Lovers

When Carly Simon asked me to shoot the cover for <u>Torch</u>, a collection of '30s and '40s songs about the struggles of love relationships, she was going through her divorce from James Taylor and was very unhappy. We had tried one shoot, but she just looked too sad. She couldn't help showing the pain she was feeling. I suggested coming back the next day to try again. I knew I had to do something to the take Carly's mind off of James. Earlier that week I'd photographed a handsome actor, Al Corley, who had told me he was a fan of Carly's. I thought he'd make a great prop. I suggested he come with me to the shoot and, if the moment was right, I'd take some pictures of them together. He was more than willing. I didn't tell Carly, I just arrived with him. I could see her spirits lift the moment they set eyes on each other. I suggested she hold on to his arm and plead with him not to leave. She must have been very convincing because he stayed for two years.

He dated my sister.

He married my friend.

He borrowed my favorite book and **never** returned it.

When he looks at me I get the feeling he understands a part of me that no one else does. It's as if we belong to the same secret society. I don't know why I feel this way. I'm pretty sure other people have had a similar experience with him. I often wonder why it is that artists who isolate themselves can get so many people to feel so close to them.

james taylor, martha's vineyard 1985

Their fans presumed them to be acid-high rock and rollers; the reality was they were health-oriented, vegetarian businessmen. Paul was a true romantic. He was always looking for Miss Right. Gene, on the other hand, did not believe that one woman could be all a man needed. He wanted to have as many women as he wanted, when he wanted them. He thought love and sex had little, if anything, to do with each other and talked about this a lot with me because he felt that I should experience the wonders of sex with him. I wanted to have sex only with someone I was in love with, someone who wanted to be monogamous. As the years passed, my kind of "perfect love" was not working out, and neither were the romantic relationships of my friends, like Paul. I started thinking I wanted to be more like Gene. His relationships were, at the very least, honest. I thought if I could have sex with someone I wasn't in love with, then maybe my romantic relationships might have a chance at lasting because there wouldn't be the same kind of emotional investment. So I told Gene I'd have sex with him. But the idea of such close physical contact without being in love made me very sad. I remember starting to unbutton my blouse and crying at the same time. Gene told me to

"forget it."

The first time I photographed her, she came to my apartment with her band. A friend of mine had left about fifteen bottles of Dom Perignon in my kitchen for safekeeping. We drank most of it, made some pictures, and talked about spiritual enlightenment.

Patti liked people to think she was androgynous. She liked them to think she was bisexual. She liked them to think she did drugs. She was one of the straightest people I knew. She'd make sure her boyfriend's laundry was done before she did a show. All she ever really wanted was a guy who she believed was an angel, then she'd support him with every ounce of energy she had.

She loved <u>Vogue</u> magazine, especially the French version. Even though she didn't have much money, she shopped at Henri Bendel, an exclusive store on Fifth Avenue. I remember a very expensive green coat she wanted. She had to have it. It was pure silk. First thing she did when we got back to her apartment was stick the coat in the washing machine. She knew how to make the look completely hers.

I talked to her almost every day. I thought she was my best friend. One afternoon I called and she told me she'd packed up everything in the apartment and was walking out the door to go live in Detroit with Fred Smith. She had met her angel and was leaving it all to be with him. I asked her to call me from Detroit. She did, thirteen years later.

patti smith, new york 1976

She'd call me up at five in the morning and say in a perky voice, "wanna go to the beach?" Patti always wore black to the beach; black pants, black shirt, and a black sweater.

patti smith, new york 1975

I met Bruce in April of 1972.

It was my first assignment for <u>Rolling Stone</u>. They told me he was the Bob Dylan of the '70s. The article was going to be called "It's Sign up a Genius Month." Because the shoot was set to take place in a bar on Bleecker Street, I knew I'd need a flash. I'd never used one before and thought this "genius" is going to know I'm stupid. Six years later Bruce told me what he was thinking the first time I took his picture. "I thought a Rolling Stone photographer, a girl who lives in New York City, she knows what she's doing. She's going to think I'm just this guy with a bar band from New Jersey. She's going to think I'm a dope."

new york 1972

One of the sexiest days in my life:

We're driving along on a cool New Jersey summer day in his 1950-something Corvette and see this burned out house. We pull over and go inside. We make photographs of each other, but the memory that stays with me more than any picture is being on my back, seeing the sky through the burned-out roof, and thinking that I was put on this earth to be with Bruce.

Once during a studio shoot Bruce started taking off his clothes. I yelled at him to stop. He thought it was funny. I was angry. I told him that if he ever took his clothes off for any photographer he'd be putting himself in the position where one day the pictures could be published.

Why did they call him "The Boss"?

He had rules of behavior and everyone was afraid to cross him. One of them was no drugs. He refused to have an opening act because he didn't want to take the chance of them influencing his band to smoke dope. He

Detroit 1978

wanted to make sure his boys were clean, so he performed long enough for two acts. I thought it was pretty funny that often after the show some of the band would sneak out behind the bus and have a joint while Bruce was still inside doing interviews or signing autographs. I don't think anyone would have believed me if I'd told them Bruce had never smoked dope. I would hear kids in the audience talk about how he must be doing cocaine to have all that energy. They were wrong. His energy came from loving what he did and being in control of it.

Bruce was upset when the Pointer Sisters had a hit with his song "Fire." It bothered him that others could have more success than he did with his own songs. He wanted a top-ten single. The major record-buying audience didn't like his low voice. When he sped up the tape on "Hungry Heart," it gave him a higher pitch. I can't remember anyone ever saying how this record didn't sound like the Bruce they'd heard up till then. Once he had that hit, mainstream radio opened up.

His music suggested the

beat of the human heart, of time ticking away. His lyrics focused on the spiritual side of erotic love and left his audience with the sense of a man brooding alone in a dark room. He created this image in pictures as well as on vinyl. He thought a lot about his look. We'd go through pictures of Dylan and talk about Bob's hair, Bob's shirt, Bob's shoes. He'd buy old clothes at Trash and Vaudeville in the Village, then make them appear even more used by running over them with the car. He never wanted me to give any magazine a picture of him smiling. The irony is that for all the deception involved in being successful, his art is based on truth.

Bruce would get on stage and tell stories like he was sitting around the living room having a few brews with his oldest friends. He used every ounce of his spirit to make the show come alive for whoever was in the audience. High-school dropouts, college PhDs, blue collar, white collar, the young and the old. It didn't matter if only five people showed for the gig. He'd go out there and perform as if his whole life depended on being his very best that night. He gave everything he had to give because rock and roll music gave him his identity. It made me love him.

Bruce told me I couldn't go three days without creating something to fight about, especially if things were going really

New Jersey 1977

ly well. The second he said it, I knew it was true. I made up things to argue over because "making up" reinforced my feeling of being loved. The way I experienced love as a child had to do with people fighting and making

up. If they didn't fight and make up, how would they know they loved each other? I fought with my sister, we fought with my mother, she fought with my grandparents, my grandparents fought with each other. I suddenly realized my concept of love was completely crazy. Bruce was right. He said it like a true friend, like he really cared about me and about us. I got a lot of self-knowledge out of our relationship. I understood that people need to be there for each other. Words are not necessary. Action is. I was not there for Bruce.

Band rehearsal, Bruce's living room, New Jersey 1977

Darkness on the Edge of Town had just been released and Bruce was in Los Angeles for a week to do shows and press. I had photo assignments in New York. He asked me to be there with him. I refused to come and screamed at him for not taking my career into consideration. I remember yelling at him on the phone every time he called. Looking back, I can say I was afraid I'd lose my identity. He was becoming very popular and I didn't want to be known as "Bruce's girlfriend." I wanted to be "Lynn Goldsmith, the photographer." He tempted me, telling me how they were going to climb this billboard on Sunset and paint over it and what great pictures I could get. I knew he felt alone and needed me, but I wouldn't go. Bruce's guitarist, Miami Steve, had a girlfriend, Maureen, who called and told me about this girl, Joyce, who kept hanging out around the band trying to get to Bruce. I didn't think anything of it. Bruce was the kind of guy who had a hard time even looking girls in the eye. Besides, I believed with all my heart that no one on this planet could be better for him than me. What I didn't take into account was that Bruce wanted to be loved when he needed it, when he asked for it, not just when I felt like it was the right time for me. I learned a big lesson. If you claim to love someone, then love them the way they ask to be loved. This pretty young thing, Joyce, who looked at him with adoring eyes while I was screaming at him about my career, hooked her fish.

How did I find out? He must have wanted me to know. We had one suitcase we shared on the road and in it I found a letter and pictures from her. I cried my heart out. He claimed he didn't want to lose me, but I couldn't stand the idea of infidelity. If only I'd known then what I know now. There are plenty of men and women who cheat on the person they're in love with and it doesn't mean they don't love the person. It simply means that they're capable of being seduced by someone or that they are seduced with the idea of a new person seeing them in an ideal light.

I break up with him. He swears undying love. I take him back and push him away again because I can't stand the thought that he was with someone else and she's there to take him in. Then I want him back and he comes back. Then I throw him out because I don't trust him, blah, blah, blah....This all leads up to the story which has been told a lot of different ways about what happened between Bruce and me at the Musicians United for Safe Energy concert at Madison Square Garden in September 1979.

Bruce and I had broken up again, this time supposedly for good. I had donated my services to MUSE when Bruce decided to perform on two nights of their shows. I didn't want either of us to be uncomfortable, but I had a job to do and I was not about to disappear because Bruce suddenly decided to be part of this

New York, 1978

cause. He came over to my apartment and we talked about how we'd handle it. He agreed not to come to the venue until ten p.m., and I agreed not to go backstage. It was his thirtieth birthday. It was Madison Square Garden. Those two facts made Bruce nervous. He once told me he would never play venues that size. He didn't believe it was good for rock and roll. The fact is, he was scared of it. He was also scared of getting old. When he came on stage he was given a birthday cake, which he threw into the audience. Later in the set he threw his harmonica into the crowd. He never would do anything like that ordinarily because he thought

New Jersey 1977

me go. He twisted harder. He pulled me up on stage to the microphone, where he said, "This is my ex-girl-friend." Then he threw me across the stage. I was humiliated. I had always expressed to Bruce how I didn't want anyone to know we were going together, how I was me, "Lynn," not "his girl-friend," and here he was announcing to everyone what he knew would upset me the most. The next day, the news-paper said I was suing for three million dollars. I would never sue Bruce. I was in a state of shock. I didn't ever want to speak to him again. I heard people say I deserved what happened to me because I was shooting when I

someone could get hurt. I knew something was wrong. I didn't know how wrong. Bruce thought he kept seeing me in the pit and he was angry. He told roadies to get me out. They looked for me but I wasn't there. I was with the film crew, shooting from about ten rows back. I didn't know there was a problem. After Jackson Browne and Tom Petty joined him at the mike, I started to pack up my camera because that was the shot we needed and I got it. The house lights were on. The crowd was standing on their chairs. I felt people tapping me on the shoulder, saying, "He wants you!" I looked up and Bruce was pointing at me from the stage, wiggling his finger for me to come to him. I shook my head no and smiled because I was scared. I knew the look in his eye when he was angry. I grabbed my camera bag and tried to head toward the back of the hall. Bruce

wasn't supposed to, trying to get unauthorized photos. I didn't even bother to respond. If I wanted unauthorized shots of Bruce, I already had him in the shower. What would I care about another concert shot! It was an insult. I knew that people wanted to see Bruce as a hero. The female photographer would have to be the wrongdoer. I thought people would soon forget about it, but until Bruce married it seemed to be the only thing a writer could latch onto as a personal moment. I was always the one at fault. I never read anything that was true from my point of view. Three years after MUSE, I was staying at the Sunset Marquis in L.A. The room above me was blasting music in the middle of the night. I called to ask them to lower it. The voice that answered the phone was Bruce. We met the next day and talked. The first thing he said was "Why'd you do it Lynnie?"

jumped from the stage and chased me. He twisted my arm behind my back. I thought he was going to break it. I pleaded for him to let

New York 1979

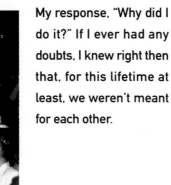

My response, "Why did I do it?" If I ever had any doubts, I knew right then that, for this lifetime at least, we weren't meant for each other.

Old love can
neither be
forgotten nor
rekindled.

I was standing in line to register for my freshman classes at the University of Michigan. I was wearing black high-heeled boots, skin-tight blue and red pin-striped bell-bottom jeans, and a studded black leather jacket. No one in Ann Arbor dressed like that. My sister had sent me the clothes from New York. I looked like I was really "hip," like I knew all about sex and drugs and rock and roll. The truth was that on the inside I was as conventional as they come. Standing in line on one side of me was a white guy with an afro and on the other side was a guy with long hair, big eyes, and a thick, navy blue striped T-shirt. It was as if a magic brush painted us in there together because all the other kids in line looked like typical Midwesterners with well-groomed hair, button-down shirts, and penny loafers. The guy with the afro spoke first, "Hi, my name is Panther," continuing with great authority and using his thumb to point to the guy next to me,

"Your name is Iggy."

He looked me deep in the eyes and said, "Your name is Famous." We became good friends and kept those names throughout college. One of us kept it from then on: Iggy. In the beginning, when the three of us hung out together, I liked Iggy as more than a friend and I knew he felt the same. One day, Panther wasn't around and we kissed. We made a plan to meet that night. Neither of us showed up. We didn't speak for about six months, until we bumped into each other on campus. We shared that we weren't as hip as we looked. We were both virgins. We became friends again. Now, when our paths cross, I feel he's kind of like a long-lost brother.

David Byrne is a perfectionist.

I had an assignment to photograph Talking Heads. After the session we talked about making images. David had this idea of being photographed with a projection of a crowd of people over him. We arranged to get together again to make the image. My camera came in handy more than once that way. I was never comfortable with people unless I thought I was doing something. With David that was easy. He wanted to make pictures. We'd shoot together once in a while and go to movies or get something to eat. I wanted to be more than his friend, but I didn't want to be the one to make the first move. Months passed before he kissed me. Shortly thereafter he asked me to go to the Yucatán. I wanted to know him better and hoped our adventure would bring us closer. We rented a car in Merida and drove across the peninsula, stopping at different pyramid sites. David had read up on Mayan culture and educated me all along the way. The trip took a week. I saw parts of his personality which were difficult for me to accept. Because of his Scottish background and my Jewish one, we had different ways of being cheap.

When we returned to New York, I felt closer to him and further from him simultaneously. I was a little scared of being with someone who lives so much in the brain. Talking Heads were scheduled to play Radio City. David told me a previous girl-friend was coming over from Japan and was going to be at the show. He asked me not to come. In a way I felt relieved. I didn't know how I felt about him, so I responded in a calm and loving manner, "Sure, I understand." An hour before the show, David came over to my house. He just wanted me to know he cared. I sent him off sweetly, telling him I was fine. At three a.m., he called to make sure everything was ok with us. I started screaming into the phone like a maniac about what a jerk he was. David never called me again. Over the years, when we've run into each other, we've talked and it's quite nice. And I've learned that yelling at someone will never make them want you to be a part of their life.

He works very hard at

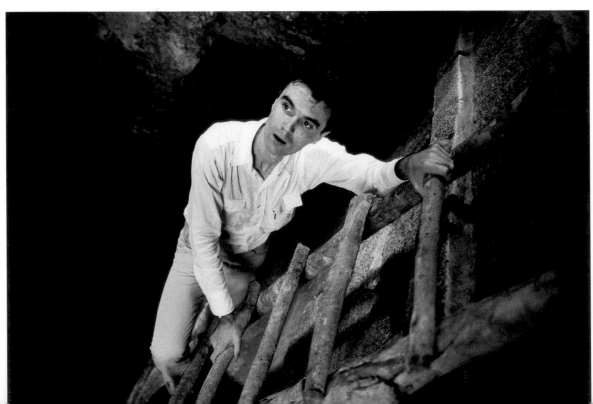

whatever he is doing.

Some people find him distant, but I think that's because they're afraid to talk to him. They think he is Mr. Super Smart, and he is. He is smart enough not to judge people. He doesn't bite. He absorbs what he can from people, then goes his own way.

Todd was one of the first people I met in New York. I was writing songs with Ralph, my sister's ex-boyfriend, who asked me to meet him at a small recording studio. Todd was underneath the board, working on the wiring. I thought he was the engineer. Ralph wasn't there yet, so we started talking. For some reason I told him about my "Monday Night Adventures." Every Monday, Woody Allen played clarinet in an Upper East Side restaurant. After the end of his set, I'd follow him wherever he went. I didn't want to talk to Woody, I just wanted to follow him because it made my heart beat really fast. Todd understood and came on some "Monday Night Adventures" with me. He became my friend and he still is. There are very few relationships which last over twenty years, especially among people in show business. Todd lives by a code with shar

lines drawn between good and bad, fair and unfair.

For him it is a world run by basic laws of reward and punishment, cause and effect. He is the only male I know who lives

successfully with two women. He has three children with them. This picture was made at his Woodstock home where I find Todd

is most comfortable.

I loved each one of them.

If anyone had ever

told me a time would

come where I'd

no longer be close

to any of them,

I wouldn't have believed it.

All three were smart, funny, and most importantly, committed to becoming educated artists. Stewart was always making off-beat short films and music of his own. He was interested in what was going on in the world politically. Sting was constantly reading. He didn't talk much. Andy was interested in painting and photography. They really motivated me, because I rarely came in contact with people interested in continually educating themselves.

I knew that any woman romantically interested in Andy or Sting would be in for a lot of heartache. They were both married and in love with really great women. They might fool around once in a while on the road, but they weren't going anywhere. I thought if I was ever going to be with one of them, it would be Stewart. He'd been living with his girlfriend, Sonya, for quite some time. I felt that she didn't really care for him. She had a son by a previous relationship and the wonderful

way Stewart looked after him made me even more sure about his character. I might have tried to get him to care for me, but I decided never to get involved intimately with any of them. I wanted to stay life-long friends.

After the four of us had been trusted confidants to each other for about five years, the situation changed. Sting separated from his wife, Andy got divorced and was living with someone, and Stewart married Sonya. I'd broken up with my boyfriend. Sting and I shared things we never had before. Against my better judgement, we became romantically involved. I thought that as much as he needed his freedom, he also needed to have a consistent "other" in his life. I didn't want to be that person. Our love evolved into another kind of love, a deeper friendship. My relationship with Andy and Stewart was never the same. And, because of that, eventually my relationship with Sting ended.

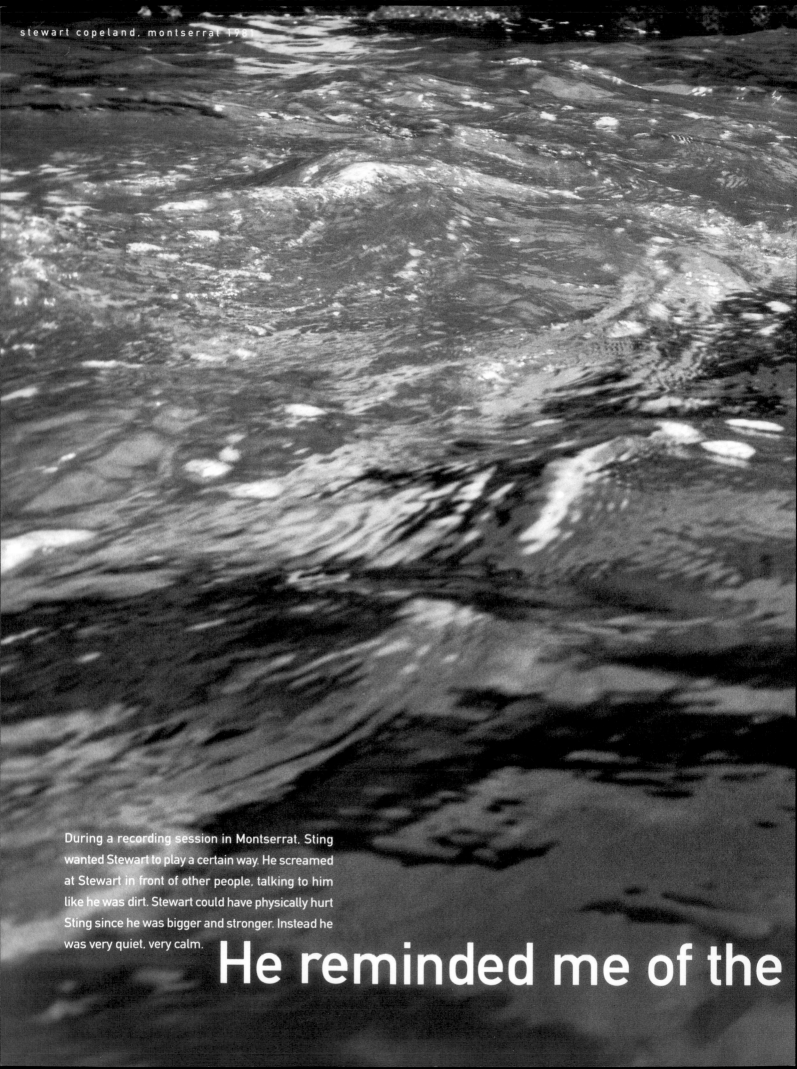

During a recording session in Montserrat, Sting wanted Stewart to play a certain way. He screamed at Stewart in front of other people, talking to him like he was dirt. Stewart could have physically hurt Sting since he was bigger and stronger. Instead he was very quiet, very calm. **He reminded me of the**

Buddha.

He was a comrade.
Because we spent so
much time together,
some people assumed
we must be having sex.
We weren't.
Andy was like a
brother to me.
We could sleep in the
same bed and
nothing happened.
I was more
comfortable with him
than with Sting or
Stewart because we
were both very clear
about having a
platonic relationship.

sting, london 1982

I had a large apartment in New York and Sting had a small room of his own there. He knew he always had a place to go where it would be like home instead of a hotel. Sometimes I wasn't even in town. I might have been at his house in London where I had my own little room.

He taught me how to make up melodies. "Get the newspaper and read it by singing it aloud."

Quite often I'm asked, "What's he like?" I answer, "He puts his pants on one leg at a time like anybody else." I'm lying by omission. Here's my real answer: he's a patient teacher and a generous human being. His intentions are good. He is, at the same time, extremely self-involved. I think he is afraid he will never live up to his own expectations.

In the mid-eighties Maria McKee introduced us in a small coffee shop in the Village. Daniel had long hair, a big fat silver ring that said "LOVE" on it, and flared jeans. I couldn't believe what a hippie he was. Sixties fashion had not come back in yet. I didn't think Daniel was ahead of his time. I thought he was way behind it. What do I know? Maybe he was both. The biggest surprise was that we became good friends. When I was growing up I knew that if some-

one liked the same kind of music as me, then in all likelihood we'd be pals. This proved true again with Daniel.

When I first meet someone, I usually have a sense of whether I will continue to know them in my personal life. This didn't happen with Mike. I thought he was young and overly influenced by his idols—Bob Dylan, Patti Smith, Van Morrison, Prince. We had a nice time making pictures. I didn't think we'd have an important relationship, but he pursued me. He told me he thought he'd written the album This Is The Sea about someone imaginary, but that it had been manifested in me! I was the girl, the woman, "the whole of the moon."

He was sure our souls were meant for each other.

We spent some time together and I felt a shift of perception. The magnitude of feeling scared me. I kept thinking how much older I was and that one day he'd leave me for someone younger. I was thirty-seven. He was twenty-five. I needed to be realistic. I pushed him away. If I could turn the clock back, I'd give it a chance.

We had been friendly for years

and I thought he was incredibly smart, funny, and musically gifted. When he came to play on my Will Powers album, I noticed he lifted his saxophone out of his case with one hand. Something seemed to be wrong with one of his arms. I asked a mutual friend what was wrong with David. He said his arm had been stunted by polio when he was a kid. David's personality as well as his playing are so strong I had never really noticed his body.

When I was seventeen I came to New York City to visit my sister. She took me to see the Mothers of Invention. I'd never heard a band like them. I became a fan. I bought all their records.

I dreamed that one day I'd meet Zappa. I did.

Thirteen years later, 1978. I was walking down 53rd Street and saw him get out of a limo and enter the Ritz Hotel. I ran home, wrote a letter requesting a photo session, and brought it back to the hotel. The letter said I'd photograph him at my cost. If he liked the pictures, I'd place them in magazines, and if he didn't like the pictures, we'd destroy them. I suggested he could always use good images of himself for press and that his time would be well spent. My mom taught me at an early age to ask for what I wanted. She'd say "If you don't get it, at least you might have had fun trying. If you don't try then you'll have regrets." Photography has taught me that if I want something from someone and I can show them how it could benefit them, I'll probably get what I want.

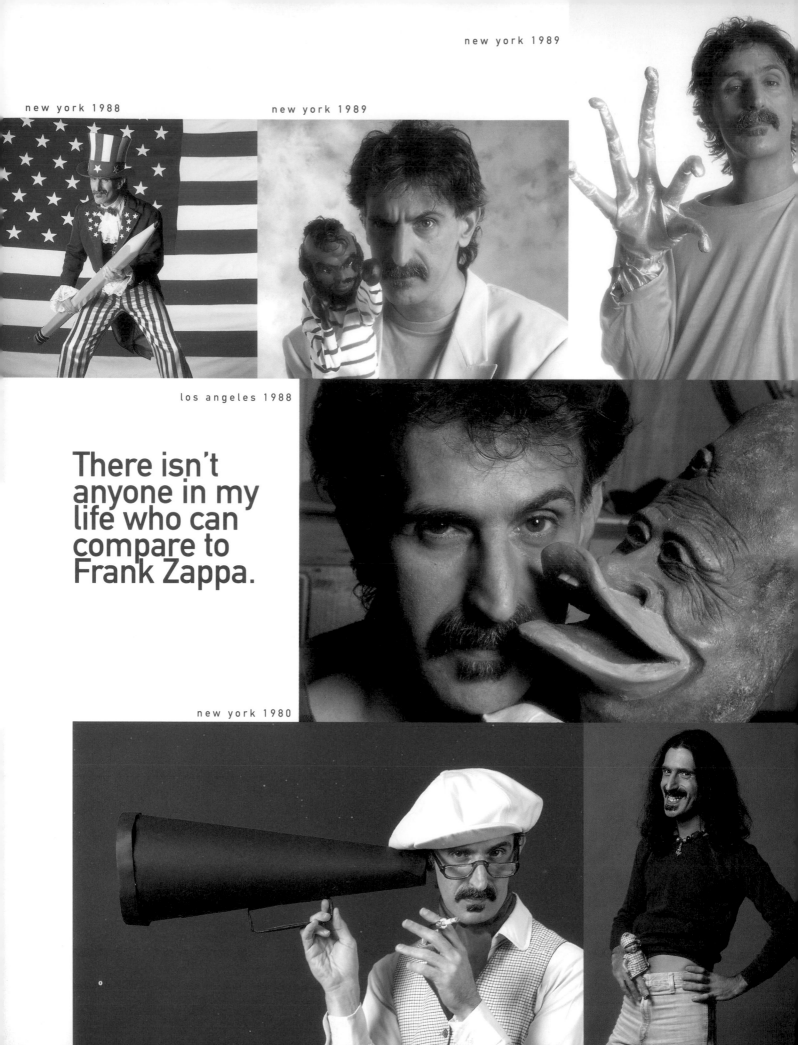

new york 1989

new york 1988

new york 1989

los angeles 1988

There isn't anyone in my life who can compare to Frank Zappa.

new york 1980

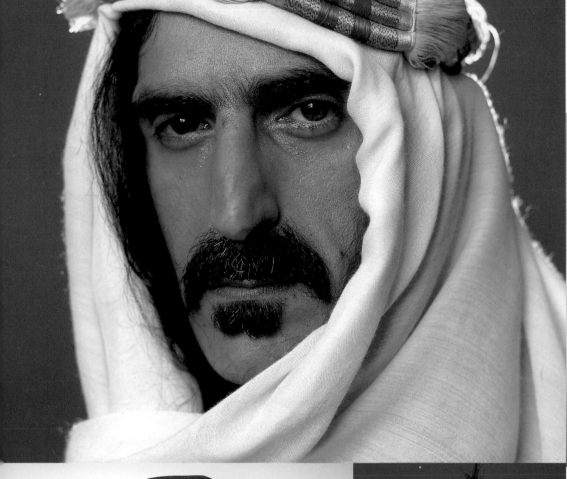

new york 1979

No one made me laugh as deeply.

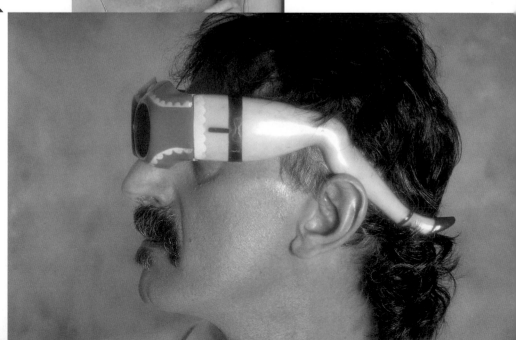

Frank loved his family. He made me feel like I was part of it. He made a lot of people feel that way.

los angeles 1979

los angeles 1988

special thanks

Glenn O'Brien, Elizabeth Van Itallie, Judith Joseph, Rachel Ruderman, David Fahey, Donna Hellman, Bobby Miller, Stephen Bishop, Robert Molnar, Merry Alpern, Bruno Masciano, Ray DeMoulin, Erika Alonso, Peter Dokus, Todd Stone, Mamiya, Canon, ICP, Roger Rubin, Nash Editions, Chris Dougherty, Laura Giammarco, Marianna Whang, Anne Beatts, Andre Grossman (for the Cypress Hill hemp background), Elizabeth White, Paul Banks, Randolph Laub, Steve & Kim Miller